PRAISE FOR REIGNITE

"*Reignite* clearly defines the DNA of top-performing sales-people and provides an outstanding road map for sales performance improvement. This is a must-read for anyone in sales or sales leadership!"

Brian Tracy
Author, High Performance Selling

"Instead of just telling salespeople what they should be doing, Kudrle and Anderson show salespeople the practical application of *Reignite* tactics and techniques. By training our North American sales force on the *Reignite* sales strategies, we have elevated the skills and attributes of our sales professionals. We now have salespeople attributing their wins to *Reignite* best practices."

Kathleen Rethelford
Sales Professional Development Manager, FIS

"*Reignite* is a great book for salespeople, sales managers, and sales executives. Scott and Chip compellingly present the case that attitude and passion are the foundation of successful selling and then provide the reader with a practical road map for building and maintaining the winning spirit. I've seen this process in action, and I know that it can be transformative for all levels of the sales team."

Craig Evanich
Senior Vice President, Chief Sales & Marketing Officer,
Andersen Windows

"I have seen firsthand how the strategies described in *Reignite* impact salespeople both professionally and personally. While many salespeople know what it takes to be successful, they aren't always willing to pay the price it takes to improve. In *Reignite,* Anderson and Kudrle clearly articulate the value proposition of 'paying the price' and provide a step-by-step guide for taking performance to the next level."

David Cronk
Vice President, Inside Sales, Hewlett-Packard

"My favorite quote from this book is: 'Most people don't fail . . . they simply give up'. *Reignite* does a great job of reminding us that if you want to 'make it happen', attitude is the first line of defense. This book also provides excellent examples on how to rebuild your skill set, capture your motivation, and discover your personal purpose and passion for selling."

Shawn O'Grady
Senior Vice President, Consumer Foods Sales Division,
General Mills, Inc.

"My sales team applied the teachings of *Reignite* at a time when our industry was at a turning point—providers were leaving the business and clients didn't know who to trust. *Reignite* re-energized the sales team and showed them how to demonstrate the importance of the relationship to our clients. The results were spectacular—we attained the number one market position the same year. And, most importantly, we have the most professional and relevant sales team in the industry. Like my team's experience, *Reignite* will take you on a journey that will truly re-energize you professionally and personally."

Patrick J. Conner
Senior Vice President, Sales and Marketing, Wells Fargo

"I have deployed the methodology in *Reignite* in two different sales organizations in the past five years, which has led to sustained sales results from my sales teams. My teams are more optimistic, more prepared, more confident, and take more responsibility for their results as a result of the teachings in this book. I recommend *Reignite* to any sales leader looking for sustained performance excellence."

Jim Dugan
Executive Vice President, Shoes For Crews; former Vice President, Global Accounts, Cintas Corporation

"As they say, a goal without measurement is merely a hope or wishful thinking. *Reignite* separates itself from other books by reinforcing the critical importance of accountability and measuring the impact of sales training. After meeting Scott and Chip many years ago and implementing the concepts in this book in my personal sales career and within my teams, the results have proven that while sales methodology is important, knowing what motivates each individual and leveraging attributes maximizes sales success. *Reignite* is a must-read for serious sales professionals and leaders who expect to win!"

Chris McNulty
Group Executive , Sales, Business Development, and Client Relations, TSYS Merchant Solutions

"In *Reignite*, Anderson and Kudrle have proven without a doubt that one's core attributes play a more important role in sales success than skills. Not only do they prove the importance of our attributes, they show you specific strategies for changing behavior. Before you read another book on selling skills, you owe it to yourself to read *Reignite!*"

Jeff Hermosillo
Vice President & General Manager, Blue Shield of California

"While there in no absence of books on selling or sales leadership in circulation today, *Reignite* truly differentiates itself among the crowd. It offers a refreshing, real-life perspective from experienced professionals on selling and what it really takes to be successful. Instead of focusing on how to sell, the authors focus on the things that really matter: why people sell, having the right or resilient attitude toward selling, and what truly motivates sales professionals to outwork their competition. This is not just a book, but rather a valuable resource that can be turned to time and again to improve your selling results and your overall sales leadership."

Mark Zesbaugh
President & CEO, Security Life Insurance Company of America

"The authors of *Reignite* take a no-nonsense approach to professional improvement that is hard to refute. I have seen the impact of their methodology on sales forces that I have led and view *Reignite* as a must-read for anyone serious about his or her career in sales."

John Caldwell
President, MLT Vacations

"This book captures the DNA of top sales performers. I've always 'hired for DNA' and 'trained for experience'. Ensuring that a team member has the right attributes and behaviors is more important than industry experience. If an individual has the right motivation, aptitude, attitude, resilience, and accountability, he will be successful. This book is a must-read for any salesperson looking to be successful and any sales leader looking to build a successful team."

Kevin Flynn
Area Vice President, salesforce.com

"This book is a must-read for anyone in sales, sales management, and even senior leadership. If you read *Reignite,* you will renew your passion for your career! I have used the strategies behind Kudrle and Anderson's methodology, and they work!"

Jim Priebe
Chief Growth Officer, Acclaris

"I have had the good fortune of knowing and working with Scott for over twenty years. Diamond Performance has always had a passion for helping individual salespeople and sales teams improve their results. *Reignite* is not only a good read for any sales professional, it's a great icebreaker for getting to know Diamond Performance. These guys can help you deliver results, which is how we are all measured."

Fred Brunk
Vice President, Sales & Marketing, Domino North America

"Having led sales organizations for more than nineteen years, I can tell you that the insights in *Reignite* are spot on! What stands in the way of every salesperson's ability to drive greater results resides in their own mind—their belief in their own ability and their attitude about the solutions they sell. *Reignite* will help you pinpoint what is standing in the way of your success and show you what to do about it."

Chris Listau
Regional Sales, Vice President, American Family Insurance

"Digital trends like social media tools, peer-to-peer communities, and social campaigns have today's sales professionals 'always on'. However, there is nothing trendy about the importance of attitude and how one's opinions, beliefs, and experiences can influence sales achievement. Scott and Chip have reawakened this important dynamic in *Reignite*—it's a must-read for sales executives regardless of their industry."

Chris Hoffmann
Senior Director & Chief Marketing Officer, Triple Tree

"The timing for the new book *Reignite* is perfect. Sales professionals do not need another book on 'how to get to the decision-maker'. They need a better understanding of what prevents them from taking their performance to the next level. *Reignite* will provide a step-by-step approach for identifying your 'personal tipping point' for success!"

Jeff Vint
Vice President Sales, Winthrop Resources
(Subsidiary of TCF Bank)

"The classic challenge in corporate sales training is measuring impact and ROI. Sales effectiveness, by contrast, takes a holistic approach to a salesperson, their motivation, skills, and organization context. Diamond Performance Group is as good a sales effectiveness consultancy as I know, anywhere. *Reignite* captures Scott's and Chip's deep knowledge, experience, and passion for helping salespeople raise their effectiveness in sales, and their personal lives, too."

Isaac Cheifetz
CEO, Open Technologies Consulting
Minneapolis Star Tribune *columnist;*
and author of The Hiring Secrets of the NFL

"In *Reignite,* Chip and Scott focus on the core attributes that drive superior sales performance. As someone who views himself as a lifelong student of sales, I have never come across a book on selling like this one!"

Steve Rice
Franchise Field Vice President,
Fortune 500 Financial Services Company

"I have read many books on selling. The biggest difference between those books and Reignite is clear: Reignite will impact you professionally as well as personally. It will force you to answer some life-changing questions about your career. And it will show you how to use these answers to truly reignite your purpose for selling."

Jim Maahs
Senior Director, Sales, Upsher-Smith Laboratories, Inc.

"In a never-ending quest to make selling pure 'science', companies will invest in the latest sales technology, methodology, and tools. And while these investments are important, the reality is this—there will always be an element of sales that is pure 'art'. Even in this world of the Internet and social media, buying and selling remains a human-to-human endeavor—people connecting with people. Reignite is a great reminder that talent, behavior, attitude, and skill still matter—perhaps today more than ever. Scott and Chip's book belongs on the desk of anyone who considers themselves a sales professional."

Jim Ninivaggi
Service Director, Sales Enablement Strategies, SiriusDecisions

"Having been in sales and sales leadership for many years, I have seen even the best salespeople lose their edge. *Reignite* will help you regain that edge and help even the new or most seasoned salesperson understand what it takes to drive business results."

Sara Sampson
Vice President, Sales & Marketing, Restaurant Technologies, Inc.

"Reignite is a great read that explains that the development of a sales force is not an event; it's a process. Scott and Chip have taken their passion for selling and put pen to paper to help explain the keys in developing a highly effective sales team. Understanding selling attributes is as important, if not more important, than skills. This book provides the framework to improve a sales force and is based on a great overall development process that is driven by data. A must-read for those trying to improve their teams."

Pete Robbins*
Vice President & General Manager, Central Area Service,
Konecranes, Inc.

*I am an employee of Konecranes, Inc. All opinions expressed are my own and do not necessarily represent the position of my employer.

"In *Reignite*, Scott and Chip remind sales professionals to rediscover and redevelop the attitudes and behaviors that have made them successful all of their lives—on the sandlot, in school, and in sales. All business is transaction—making offers, closing sales, and delivering on promises. This book is a must-read for business professionals who want to maintain their selling passion over the whole of their careers."

Brian Irion
Partner, Aon Hewitt

"Even Honda lawnmowers need to have their blades sharpened! So do we! Scott and Chip have put it all together in *Reignite*. Their experience, methods, and delivery are topnotch. They helped my team come together and improve performance."

Michael Hussey
Vice President, Business Development, Pearson

"I have worked with sales organizations for over twenty years on providing improved research, systems, and process analysis to make better go-to-market decisions. However, none of that matters if the individuals in a sale organization do not practice 'brilliance in the basics' of attitude, behavior, motivation, accountability, and integrity. Scott and Chip lay out a strong case for understanding the importance of these attributes and developing them in each and every one of the sales team members. It is the only way to create sustainable, predictable, and dependable sales performance. The deep content of this book is not only developed through their work with a variety of companies, but Scott and Chip have lived it 'out loud' in their own professional and personal lives. This is a book that every person in sales should read, internalize, and then act upon. Every sales leader should use this as their playbook as they coach and direct their teams."

Kurt M. Schroeder
Principal, Growth Strategies, Baker Tilly Virchow Krause, LLP

"*Reignite* explains why behaviors are the drivers of high sales performance and a necessary complement to traditional selling skills."

Steve Snyder
Vice President of a multinational company

"Scott and Chip offer valuable insights on how to combine the power of great people with great process to build sustainable success. The increased focus on sales process has dramatically improved the effectiveness and productivity of today's sales professional. However, it takes a team of highly motivated individuals to truly stand out in a marketplace where every sales organization is becoming more disciplined. *Reignite* will help you unleash your most valuable asset—your people."

Jeff Barovich
Senior Vice President, Forrester Research

"*Reignite* addresses the ongoing challenge in sales, which is maintaining your motivation and will to succeed throughout the ups and downs of a sales career. Whether you are just starting out in sales or have a twenty-five-year career, you will find this book to be very inspiring!"

Eric Nuytten, CEBS, REBC
Senior Vice President, Senior Benefits Consultant, Associated Financial Group, LLC.

"We applied the concepts in *Reignite* with our team in a very difficult business environment. The approach is both qualitative and quantitative, and, when applied, their concepts and step-by-step approach will improve results."

Leon Monroe, CLU,ChFC
Vice President, Business Development, The Hartford

"Loaded with actionable ideas, *Reignite* is a refreshingly candid perspective from the front lines of selling in today's competitive environment. High performers seek continuous improvement, and this book certainly will be sought after by those who aspire to be the best in their field."

W. Thomas McEnery
Fortune 25 Chief Marketing Officer

"Absolutely loved this book! Scott and Chip are two 'high integrity professionals' that have a proven methodology of delivering results. I have personally experienced their passion for success and finding attributes in a sales team to improve results. As a manager of others, I love this methodology because it will improve behaviors that deliver success . . . it is measurable and sustainable."

Tim Burns
Vice President, Institutional Corporate Accounts Central, Ecolab

REIGNITE

How to Rekindle Your
PASSION for SELLING

SCOTT ANDERSON   **CHIP KUDRLE**

DEDICATION

From Scott

This book is dedicated to my family. First of all, to my children, Cole and Tess, you have helped me understand God's love more than any previous life experience. Someday you will be able to understand my love for you when you have children of your own. You have been a blessing every day of my life.

To my wife, Ami, thank you for making life fun, exciting, and fulfilling. Without your continued love and support, this book and my business would not have been possible.

To my parents, Marge and LeRoy "Andy" Anderson, thank you for the wonderful foundation you provided. From the safe and loving childhood and the strong Christian values you lived to demonstrating a strong work ethic to help us all persevere as adults. I am eternally grateful!

From Chip

To my parents, Bob and Mary, who instilled principles in me that I try to teach to my own kids— Natalie, Alison, and Aaron. Principles that I hope are evident in this book.

To my brothers and sisters (all eight of you!). Thank you for your love, friendship, and guidance through life and for picking up where our parents left off.

Finally, to my wife, Patti, who has been a great partner in life. She unwaveringly manages her own professional career and our family while I am oftentimes jumping from city to city, coaching and training sales professionals. Without your support, my work and the work on this book would not have been possible.

CONTENTS

CONTENTS

FOREWORD
DR. ALAN R. ZIMMERMAN

IN THE MOVIE, *A LEAGUE OF THEIR OWN,* the baseball coach talked to his dispirited team, saying, "Of course, it's hard. If it wasn't hard, everybody would do it!"

That's the way it is with selling. It can be hard. I suppose that's why the bookstores are filled with books on selling. Every salesperson wants to know the "secret."

After speaking to more than twenty-five hundred audiences around the world, and having maintained a 92 percent repeat and referral business for more than two decades, I can tell you there isn't a "secret." There isn't a magical set of words you can use or questions you can ask that will guarantee your success in sales.

And that's the problem with so many sales books and sales courses. They miss the key point in selling—that *your success in sales has a lot more to do with what is happening in your head than what is coming out of your mouth.*

That is what so refreshing—and dare I say, reigniting—about Scott and Chip's book *Reignite*. They don't miss that key point. They get it. They really do.

You see, it doesn't matter if we're in the midst of good economic times or challenging ones. You can still be successful in sales if you think the right way and then behave accordingly.

Along those lines, I've found four "best sales practices" that have worked extraordinarily well for me, and I believe they will do the same for you. As you read, study, and apply the lessons from *Reignite,* you'll see that these practices "reinforce" Scott and Chip's recommendations perfectly.

1. Keep on Believing

Believe in yourself. Believe in the value of your sales profession. Believe in your product. Believe in your service. Believe in your customers. Believe in a power bigger than yourself. And believe you can be successful.

That's what Mary Kay, the founder of Mary Kay Cosmetics, did. She went through enormous challenges and came out a sales winner because she learned, "One of the secrets of success is to refuse to let temporary setbacks defeat us." Just keep on believing that success is on the way.

That's what Lee Iacocca, the former chairman of the Chrysler Corporation, did. When the world told him to let his debt-ridden company die, Iacocca refused. He didn't wait for the economy to change or for a government bailout to rescue him. Iacocca believed in himself, in his company, in his products, and in his workers. He pronounced, "So what do we do? Anything—something. So long as we don't just sit there. If we screw it up, start over. Try something else. If we wait until we've satisfied all the uncertainties, it may be too late."

2. Work Hard

There's no substitute for hard work. Simply put, there "ain't no free lunch."

When I look at highly successful salespeople, I think, "It's no wonder they're doing so well. Look at everything they're doing."

Could the same thing be said about you? If someone were to follow you around for a week and painstakingly record everything you did to advance your sales career, would that person walk away with a long list of all the things you're doing to get ahead? Or would that person have a long list of the excuses you gave and the times you wasted?

Sometimes people fool themselves into thinking they're putting out a 100 percent effort—when in reality, they're not. For example, many salespeople aren't doing too well these days, and I've often heard them say, "I sent out one hundred flyers announcing our new product line, and I didn't get any response. I did everything I could."

One hundred percent effort means that you've exhausted every possible opportunity for reaching your goal. If you're looking for a sale, 100 percent effort would include researching individual companies that are a great fit for your product or service, sending these companies personalized letters and e-mails, and calling to follow up with intelligent, company-specific questions—not to mention networking, referrals, and a host of other selling strategies.

If you were looking for a job, 100 percent effort means telling a potential boss, "I'm sure you've got a lot of applicants here. But I believe so strongly in my ability to meet your needs, I'll work for you for thirty days with no pay. Let me prove to you my ability. In thirty days, evaluate my performance. If it's not up to par, let me go. But when I prove myself to you, I expect to be given the job and paid for the thirty days of work."

Now that's putting in 100 percent effort! And that's what you need to do to succeed in sales or any other area of your life—because success is more often the result of attitude and hard work than plain old talent all by itself.

3. Practice Endurance

To many salespeople, "endurance" is a nasty word. They would like to come by success the "easy" way. They want it to fall into their laps.

But that's an extremely rare occurrence. Most of the time, 99.99 percent of the time, success comes AFTER you "endure" awhile. And all the greats in every field of endeavor have learned how to "endure."

As professional tennis player, Bjorn Borg noted, "My greatest point is my persistence. I never give up in a match. However down I am . . . I fight until the last ball. My list of matches shows that I have turned a great many so-called irretrievable defeats into victories."

Could the same be said of you? That you never give up? That you endure?

Or do people say you bail out when selling gets a little tough? Do they say you give up way too easily and throw in the towel too quickly? Do they point out the fact that you seldom finish what you start?

If you answer "yes" to any of the questions in the previous paragraph, remember the words of John Quincy Adams. He noted, "Patience and perseverance have a magical effect before which difficulties disappear and obstacles vanish." In other words, there's power in perseverance.

Of course, that's easier said than done. So you've got to . . .

4. Stay Committed

Everything else being equal, commitment wins every time. So fight back any feelings of discouragement that might get in your way. Don't allow yourself to hang it up when things get rough.

If you're going to be successful, you've got to remember the letters M.I.H.—just like that one high school kid. He had a passion for his favorite sport of wrestling. And last year he won the second place trophy in the state championships.

Now he could have thought that was good enough. But the day after the state finals, he was back in the same old gym, working out in the same old sweats with one small change. He had placed white tape on each of his three middle fingers, and on each piece of tape was a letter—M.I.H.

He kept the letters on his fingers all year, and he trained harder than ever, until he again found himself at the state tournament. This time he was crowned state champion.

Of course, people wanted to know how he did it. He created a tool that helped him focus, stay the course, and keep up his commitment. He knew that, if he really wanted to be the best, it was up to him. He was determined to M.I.H.—Make It Happen.

I believe Scott and Chip have written a book that will help you Make It Happen. I've known them for years, as my students, as my teaching assistants, and as my colleagues. I respect their knowledge, admire their skill, and applaud their integrity.

As you pursue your goals, as you strive toward greater sales success, follow these four points, and you will not only survive . . . but thrive. After all, most salespeople don't fail. They just give up.

Dr. Alan Zimmerman speaks to organizations seeking to transform the people side of their business. His keynotes and seminars focus on the communication, motivation, leadership, and teamwork that pay off in bigger profits and better relationships—on and off the job. To learn more about his work, check out his website at www. DrZimmerman.com or e-mail him at Alan@DrZimmerman. com.

IS YOUR ATTITUDE IN THE RIGHT PLACE TO BE SUCCESSFUL?

"If a man is called to be a street sweeper, he should sweep streets even as Michelangelo painted, or Beethoven composed music, or Shakespeare wrote poetry. He should sweep streets so well that all the hosts of heaven and earth will pause to say, here lived a great street sweeper who did his job well."

MARTIN LUTHER KING JR., CIVIL RIGHTS LEADER

PEOPLE RARELY SET OUT TO BE IN SALES. When we talk to tenth graders on career day in Twin Cities schools, we always ask: What are your career aspirations? What do you want to do when you grow up? The number one career ambition, in our experience, among Minnesota schoolchildren is marine biologist. Really, how many marine biologists does the world need?

Admittedly, a show of hands in a general discussion on a pleasant day in a classroom is not a scientific survey. But still, we seldom hear a child express a burning desire for a career in sales or account management. It is not as sexy sounding as a marine biologist or professional athlete. And yet, we know that a healthy portion of these students will end up in some sort of selling profession.

Here is our point: Most of us have fallen into our careers. But in the case of those of us who are successful, our careers have gotten inside of us.

That's why we wrote this book: to show you how to be successful in any career—whether it is swimming with the dolphins on the high seas or treading water with the sharks in high finance—but especially we want to help you succeed brilliantly in sales.

We are sales guys. We have been in the trenches. We have had successful sales careers. And now we run Diamond Performance Group. Since 1991, we have been in the field training the best salespeople from the best organizations in the world: IBM, HP, The Hartford, United Health Group, New York Life, and American Express to name a few. Although based in Minneapolis, we travel all over the world helping companies develop successful sales teams. We are trainers and coaches, and we get results.

Unlike many trainers, however, we do not focus only on skills. This is not a book about developing your selling skills; there are already hundreds of books on how to close the sale. Our expertise is helping you define the attributes you need to become a top performer—to really get in touch with your successful inner salesperson.

Can You Improve Your Attitude?

If you want to be successful in any career, you have to commit to excellence. This is extremely important in selling where the individual needs to find the link between what he or she sells and the ultimate value of the product or service to the customer. Salespeople need to feel that what they are doing is important. Sales is not like many professions, where you can hide in an isolated cubicle and do your job. Salespeople have to get out and get their nose bloodied every day facing rejection and challenges with both current customers and new prospects.

If you are not tied into a strong sense of purpose in your career, you are destined to be an average performer or, worse yet, an underperformer headed for professional job switcher. To the underperformer, the grass is always greener on the other side. Even top performers who lose their drive have to continually remind themselves of why they do what they do.

But let's imagine that you could change all that—simply by improving your attitude. Remember, sales is a numbers game. You could make a change that moves the needle on the scale of success by a mere 10 percent and have a huge jump in sales. What did you do? You changed your behavior, your attitude, and your motivation.

What Makes Top Performers Unique?

Just as the job gets into top performers, top performers get into the job. They find purpose or value in what they do. They love their jobs. They are engaged employees and want to be the best.

We all look at success differently and work at it differently, but at the core, we all need to feel relevant and that we are making a contribution that matters.

Top performers position themselves mentally to succeed. They find their own unique ways of moving up the ladder of success by having the right attitude, being more motivated, practicing personal accountability, and treasuring integrity.

What We Hope You Gain from This Book

We wrote *Reignite* with two purposes in mind:

1 **Increasing your sales effectiveness regardless of the selling methodology you or your company uses.** We recognize that bookstores are chock-full of the newest and greatest selling and account management methodologies (essentially saying the same thing in different ways). In this book, we will highlight the success factors that are absolutely critical to increasing your performance, based on our experiences coaching and training salespeople for more than twenty years.

2 **Enhancing both your personal and business journey.** The topics we will be discussing can change your life, and the changes won't stop at the office door. We will be providing real-life examples and strategies to help you move into real change, and that will ripple through all aspects of your life.

It's amazing what a change in attitude can do. Right out of college, we decided to form a team of friends to play Thursday night D league softball. Most of our friends on the team were athletes (maybe athlete is too strong of a word . . . you know who you are); some were even baseball players. At the end of the first season, we found ourselves at the bottom of the standings. We couldn't understand how such a group of talented ballplayers (maybe we were poor at self-assessment) in a D league could continue to lose.

At the end of a frustrating season, one of our colleagues made an insightful observation. He boldly announced that we should move up to the B league the following year. When we all looked at him in shock, he quickly pointed out, "We can lose to better teams than this."

And it worked. Our softball team did move up to a higher league and found years of success competing against better competition. Our skills didn't change all that much over the years, but our attitude did.

Somehow, this book found its way to you. Give it a chance; don't let it sit on the bookshelf unopened and unread. We hope it will help you improve your performance, increase your job satisfaction, and make a difference in your life.

Enjoy!

CHAPTER 1

KEYS TO SUCCESS: REALLY CHANGING BEHAVIOR

Pareto Principle: 80 percent of production volume usually comes from 20 percent of the producers.

**VILFREDO PARETO,
NINETEENTH-CENTURY ECONOMIST**

THE WHOLE REASON YOU PICKED UP THIS BOOK was to become a more effective salesperson, or, if you are a sales manager, to build a more successful sales team. Have you been through a ton of skills training but haven't seen the performance results you would like? We'll let you in on a little secret: skills-based training doesn't matter if your attributes aren't there.

Why someone is successful is not about training or methodology. If the key to top performance was great skill-based training, we would all be leading the pack. But we're not. Every sales team has top performers, moderate performers, and underachievers. And most likely, everyone on the sales team has received the same training. So how can the top performers consistently overachieve their goals and objectives, while the moderate performers often underachieve their goals, and the underachievers significantly underachieve their goals?

What makes the difference?

The top performer is able, and willing, to apply his training to execute a strategy.

In many instances, the ability to execute requires an individual to challenge his old paradigms or comfort zones. It requires leaving the place where you feel safe and stepping off the path of least resistance (old patterns)—and learn. We know the best indicator of future behavior is one's past behavior. If you want to improve your results, you have to embrace a new paradigm or set of rules.

Most top performers are consistently trying new ideas and strategies outside their comfort zone, which helps them to *greatly increase the size of their comfort zones*. That is why a company that invests in training—and especially if the training is good, edgy, and differentiates—will see a greater return on its investment (ROI) with top performers. The top performer will leverage the experience and get better. For the moderate performer and underachiever, on the other hand, training can result in little change because they stay in their comfort zones or lack the awareness for the need to change.

Why Training Doesn't Improve Performance

Why do some individuals fail to improve their performance through training? Many times the company has not addressed the numerous barriers that get in the way of execution. John Wooden, UCLA Hall of Fame basketball coach who at one time had an eighty-eight-game winning streak and won ten national championship titles, said, "It is what you learn after you know it all that counts." Essentially, is the individual open to learning? Being open to new ideas and improving is the first step.

There are numerous barriers to getting someone to use his sales methodology (training), challenge his old paradigms, and execute a successful sales strategy—all of which are needed to become a top performer. Let's look at the Effectiveness illustration in figure 1.

There are four bubbles:

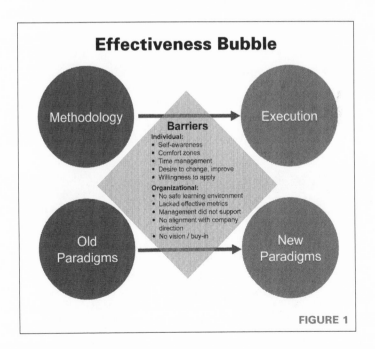

Effectiveness Bubble

Methodology → Execution

Barriers

Individual:
- Self-awareness
- Comfort zones
- Time management
- Desire to change, improve
- Willingness to apply

Organizational:
- No safe learning environment
- Lacked effective metrics
- Management did not support
- No alignment with company direction
- No vision / buy-in

Old Paradigms → New Paradigms

FIGURE 1

- **Methodology:** Think of methodology as all of the sales training you've ever had, all of the business books you've ever read, all of the audio CDs on selling you've ever listened to. Methodology equates to the "know-how" of selling.

- **Execution:** This refers to your ability to take the training you have been given, the "know-how" of selling, and actually apply it in real-life selling situations. As you might expect, this is where things break down. Think of all the training you've had and ask yourself: honestly, how much of it have you actually internalized? The reason most salespeople never reach "execution" is due to personal barriers that they have not yet addressed.

- **Old Paradigms:** This is your old way of doing things as you sit in your cozy comfort zone.

- **New Paradigms:** This is an exciting place where you have faced your barriers, made adjustments, enlarged your comfort zone, and see a whole new world open to you. This is where top performers live and are able to apply new strategies and tactics.

Now, you can improve your effectiveness by moving from methodology to execution and from your old paradigm to your new one, but it's not an easy trip. You will have to traverse mountains and ford rivers. The top performers love this stuff; in fact, they've already figured out their barriers and how to overcome them. However, if your performance has slipped recently, discerning what your barriers are and working on ways to overcome them is your ticket to returning to the realm of top performance.

Individual Barriers to Success

Let's take a moment and look at the barriers we commonly see in our work with major companies. We break the barriers down into individual and organizational. You probably have little control over the organization so we'll save that discussion for another book. Our focus in this book is on the individual challenges:

- **Self-awareness:** The challenge here is that the same set of skills that are required for competency are the same set of skills that are required to *recognize incompetency.* When we are performing at a moderate level, the biggest barrier we may face is that we don't view our skills, attributes, and performance in an accurate light. (See chapter 3 for more on self-awareness.)

- **Comfort zones:** An unwillingness to step out of your comfort zone is a huge barrier because that is the way you accept a new paradigm and get more out of your training. We saw many examples of this while coaching a national account management team in a large telecommunications company. Because of the changing business environment and the proliferation of competition, this company needed its account managers to step up their game: doing a better job getting to senior-level decision makers (protecting their existing client relationships) and going beyond their day-to-day contacts to meet new people (identifying opportunities). These two strategies stretched the comfort zone of many of the account managers. As one said, "This isn't what I signed up for when I took this job!" With that prevailing attitude, all of the sales methodology in the world isn't going to help many of these account managers elevate their game, until they have effectively addressed their barriers.

◆ **Time management:** No one has enough time. We travel, run from meeting to meeting, have 110 e-mails a day to answer, spend hours reacting to customer service issues, and still must have the energy to spend quality time with our family. Time management is an easy term to throw around, but does it get to the essence of what is really holding you back? Often you need to dig deeper. Is it a work/family balance issue? Is it a conscious decision to put family ahead of your desire to improve professionally? Or are you simply not willing to pay the price for improvement? No one is trying to tell you what your priorities should be, but you need to be honest about what is truly holding you back.

◆ **Lack a desire to change and improve:** Why do you want to get better or change? If you figure out the "why"—fear of losing your job, the desire for financial rewards and recognition, your need to compete—you will be more likely to thrive in the process of change. We asked one IBM executive what he attributed his success to. He said, "I hate to lose, whether it's a business deal or playing Monopoly with my family. Losing gnaws at me."

◆ **Unwillingness to apply your training:** This is the deal breaker. If you are afraid of making mistakes, find practice boring and so have no desire to prepare to get better, or are no longer engaged in your career, you probably won't make the effort to apply your sales training. You have decided to take the path of least resistance and maintain status quo.

CONFUSING PROGRESS WITH ACTIVITY

Some salespeople are so mired in activities that they fail to take a step back to see if actual progress is being made. They feel good at the end of the day or week with the number of tasks they have completed without assessing if they are really the right tasks. It is easy to get stuck performing "red light" activities such as wrangling internal reports, expense reports, and reactive e-mail rather than "green light" activities that drive progress toward goal achievement such as attending networking events to identify new opportunities, blocking off prospecting time on your schedule to set appointments, or even as simple as ensuring that you are meeting with actual decision makers. Are you contacting individuals who have the power to say yes or filling your calendar with go-nowhere meetings with purchasing agents and other middle management influencers? Get off the work treadmill, examine what you do, and see if you can get more impact from your tasks. Reduce "red light" activities and amp up your "green light" activities. You will see a difference in your sales.

True Cost of Effectiveness

This book stresses that top performers have four key attributes: attitude, integrity, motivation, and accountability. Individuals who possess more of those attributes are more likely to embrace skills-based training, which makes them a better investment for the company when it comes to cost-effective training and also means they can increase their personal effectiveness more easily with training.

Individuals with fewer of these attributes will find it more difficult to use traditional skills development training as a way to increase effectiveness. The cost of effectiveness is extremely high for individuals who have none of these key attributes. A company may never receive ROI from giving these individuals skills training.

What does all this mean for you? A company has to have skilled employees. The more sophisticated the sales position, the more advanced (or unique) skills are required. A company will seek to acquire these advanced skills in three ways: recruit the best talent, provide training opportunities, or let the sales team learn from trial and error.

If you do not have the attributes to use your training to take your effectiveness to another level, are you likely to be offered training and growth opportunities in your company? Will you be considered an asset or deadwood?

Your future may depend on the very attributes we will be talking about in this book.

"The people who get on in this world are the people who get up and look for the circumstances they want, and, if they can't find them, make them."

GEORGE BERNARD SHAW, WRITER

REFLECTION EXERCISES

What are your biggest barriers to taking your performance to the next level? Tip: Focus on those barriers you have complete control over.

What old paradigms (i.e., negative thought patterns) do you need to rid yourself of? What new paradigms do you need to embrace?

CHAPTER 2

THE TOP PERFORMER'S TIPPING POINT

"Watch your thoughts because they become your beliefs."

VINCE LOMBARDI, FOOTBALL COACH

SOMETIMES WE HAVE FUNNY IDEAS ABOUT WHAT WILL increase our effectiveness. A golfer, for example, may swear that the newest and latest driver will surely change his game. A writer may believe that she can write the great American novel, if only she buys a new computer. A salesperson may insist that he would be a top performer, if only the company would lower its prices.

All of these excuses are based on external barriers: a poor golf club, an old computer, high prices. We spend a lot of time obsessing over the external barriers, when working on our internal barriers would get us much farther.

---

*"History has demonstrated that the most notable
winners usually encountered heartbreaking obstacles
before they triumphed. They won because they
refused to become discouraged by their defeats."*

B.C. FORBES, FINANCIAL JOURNALIST, FOUNDER OF *FORBES*

The Difference Between High and Low Performers

Do you have what it takes to be a top performer? And if
you don't, how do you get what it takes?

In our informal polling of sales professionals, we have
found the key characteristics of high and low performers:

High Performers

◆ Are resilient

◆ Are optimistic

◆ Are goal oriented

◆ Love challenges

◆ Like competition

◆ Focus on continued improvement

◆ Are highly skilled

◆ Enjoy leading the team

◆ Seek new ways of doing things

Low Performers

◆ Are unable to prioritize

- Blame others

- Feel overwhelmed

- Feel helpless and lack confidence

- Think of work as a job

- Bounce from company to company

- Talk a big game

- Use a small percentage of their capabilities

- Become defensive

- Do not understand the "big" picture

- Give effort that far outweighs the result

- Are not open to new ideas

- Are passionless

As you review this list, think of people you know who are top performers. Do they exude some of these characteristics? Top performers often have a calm confidence that goes with these traits. Boston Celtic great Bill Russell once said before a game, "The game is scheduled; we have to play it; we might as well win." He was referring to the monotony of a long season and that attitude you need to make an effort to win every game. It's no different in sales. You have to go to work so you might as well give your best effort.

Oddly enough, low performers are confident as well—confident they are giving 100 percent, when they really are not. Their sales numbers prove it. While top performers come into training eager to learn new strategies and end up getting the most out of training, low performers think they know it all already. "Why do I need to take time out of my busy day for this?" they ask. We have seen it so many times over the years it is predictable. During the first break of a training workshop, a low performer will walk up to the instructor, slap him on the back, and say, "This is great stuff, but I am already doing this." Then over the course of a two-day workshop we will see that same salesperson in role plays and recognize that he really isn't using the selling strategies we are teaching. He's just talking a big game. And when he hasn't achieved his sales goals, whose fault is it? Not his, he says. As we will discuss in later chapters, one of the characteristics of a low performer is that he blames others for his inadequacies.

LACK OF CONVICTION CAN STALL YOUR PROGRESS

We were hired by a company to train its 120 account managers in presentation skills. To our amazement, most of them did not believe that presenting was part of their job. They insisted that they were doing just fine sitting down with customers and chatting with them. They didn't see the value in learning how to make a powerful presentation—standing on their feet. They lacked conviction and were afraid to step out of their comfort zone. This is not surprising since the fear of public speaking is the number one phobia in the US. Eventually, we succeeded in persuading them that presentation skills were important to their job. In fact, a University of Minnesota study says you are 43 percent more persuasive as a presenter when you stand up to give your presentation. You are not only more likely to nail the sale, but your customers are likely to pay 26 percent more for the same product.

The Tipping Point in Sales Performers

You do not have to be strong in all areas to be a top performer, just in enough of them to reach a "tipping point" of success. This was established by the work of David McClelland, a Harvard professor and thought leader on human motivation and emotional intelligence. In his study of top performers, he used the term "tipping point," which actually is a chemistry term for when you add enough of the right ingredients to create a chemical reaction.

McClelland found that stars are not just talented in a few areas such as initiative or influence but have strengths across the board. They must master a mix of competencies from each of the five emotional intelligence areas: self-awareness, self-regulation, motivation, empathy, and social skills.

They will be successful when they are strong in enough of these competencies to reach critical mass for success or the tipping point. "Once you reach the tipping point," McClelland said, "the probability of your performance being outstanding shoots up."

Over years of observation and researching top sales performers, we have developed our own Tipping Point Model for sales success. It has proven to drive performance improvement for our clients, and it can do the same for you.

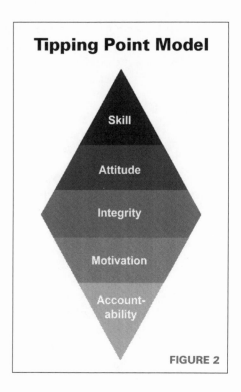

The model (see figure 2) can be broken down into these areas:

- **Skill:** Depending on the selling environment, this is a complex skill set, a transactional skill set, or a mix of the two. Essentially, it comes down to a simple question: is the salesperson making it easy for the customer to say yes?

- **Attitude:** What puts the salesperson in the right frame of mind to do his job? What puts him in the wrong frame of mind to make the sale? Attitude is impacted by several things:

❖ *Optimism*—How optimistic is the salesperson? How does the salesperson explain negative events to himself?

❖ *Self-confidence*—Salespeople are only human. They do the things they are confident in and avoid the things they are not confident in.

❖ *Comfort zone*—How often is the individual challenging his comfort zone on a weekly basis? If a person is not challenging his comfort zone, he is not getting better. We know top performers have expanded their comfort zones by trying new ideas and strategies. And by having bigger comfort zones, they are willing to try even more new ideas or strategies to improve their performance or enhance their chances of landing the deal. This is what growth is about—constantly expanding your comfort zone.

◆ **Motivation:** The driving force is different for every top performer. Do you understand what your driving force is? We typically divide motivation into three driving forces for the individual.

❖ *Punitive*—the old stick, which is fear of failure, not making quota, or getting fired.

❖ *Prize*—which is motivation by financial rewards, recognition, or material things.

❖ *Purpose*—which is why you do your job. For example, "I do my job because it is my responsibility; I need to support my family" or "I do my job because I love it."

◆ **Accountability:** Essentially, you own it! You are responsible for your business results and your personal development. Top performers focus on what they can control and do not worry about the things that are outside of their control.

◆ **Integrity:** Are you building trusting relationships with your customers or prospects? Integrity in our model is whatever you are doing to build trust or what you are doing to detract from a trusting relationship. Integrity often is displayed in simple ways: showing up on time (calendar integrity), returning phone calls in a timely manner, asking effective questions, and listening (people want salespeople to lead them into the right decision). Do your behaviors build trust or detract from it?

As we discussed, top performers do not have to be strong in all of these categories. They do need, however, enough of these attributes and skills to reach a tipping point of success. Ironically, everyone's formula is different.

We conducted a survey with executives to determine the makeup of their top performers within their organization using our Tipping Point Model. We asked: if someone consistently performs in the top 20 percent of an organization for a period of time, why are they performing at that level? We surveyed executives in numerous large to mid-size companies including Motorola, Kodak, and UnitedHealthcare and presented this data at the Strategic Accounts Managers Association (SAMA) annual conference.

The results might surprise you. When we asked what role do skills and attributes play in someone's success, the executives ranked them:

- Attitude: 26%

- Motivation: 22%

- Accountability: 20%

- Integrity: 19%

- Skills: 13%

Based on this survey, skills was consistently the least important factor in one's success formula. But where do all the corporate training dollars go to? Skills!

There is no doubt that top performers have good selling skills. But how did they acquire them? We believe there are factors in play here having to do with attributes. If an individual is strong in attitude, motivation, integrity, and accountability, he will seek out and invest in himself to get the skills he needs to be successful. Also, if an individual has the attributes we are discussing, he will get more out of any training the company provides. So top performers seek out skills and use them more effectively.

The survey also gave us a peek into what executives value in various attributes and what critical behaviors they consider important in their employees. Here are a few of the top ones in the order of importance:

- *The most critical behaviors of attitude:* resilient, confident, wants to win

- *The most critical behaviors of integrity:* delivers on commitments, reliable, ethical

- *The most critical behaviors of motivation:* disciplined, goal driven, desires to succeed

- *The most critical behaviors of accountability:* accepts responsibility for results, takes ownership of both internal and external issues, does not rely on excuses

To become a top performer, it is not all about what you learn (the training or methodology). It is about who you are and what you do with what you know. That's where attributes come in. Work on your attributes, and you soon will be at your own tipping point for sales success.

"People seldom see the halting and painful steps by which the most insignificant success is achieved."

ANNIE SULLIVAN, TEACHER OF HELEN KELLER

CHAPTER 3

ARE YOU READY TO IMPROVE?

"One of life's most painful moments comes when we must admit that we didn't do our homework, that we are not prepared."

MERLIN OLSEN, FOOTBALL STAR, BROADCASTER, ACTOR

TO INCREASE YOUR COMPETENCY, YOU HAVE TO BE aware of your need to change and be willing to act. When we work with companies, we have the sales managers conduct an initial assessment on each individual on their team. This helps us form a strategy for improving team and individual performance.

Our first step is to help companies categorize performance levels. Where do team members fall? Are they top performers, moderate performers, or underperformers?

Our second step is to understand each rep's readiness for improvement. Most people go through five stages of readiness:

1 **Oblivious:** They cannot see a problem. They resist any attempt to help them change.

2 **Contemplation:** They recognize the need for change (improvement) but substitute thinking for acting.

3 **Preparation:** They have begun to focus on the solution, on how to improve, and are eager to develop an action plan. This is many times propelled to a heightened stage by an event such as being put on a performance plan.

4 **Action:** Visible change begins. They embrace the plan and start practicing expected behaviors.

5 **Adoption:** They are consistent in behaviors which have now become habits. There is little chance of relapse.

Incidentally, most companies go through the same process when making a decision to either purchase a new product or replace an existing vendor. It is virtually impossible to improve performance or win a deal if the person or business is in the oblivious state. You must help them understand the need for improvement.

It's a simple process, and here's how it works. Let's say Tony picks up his clothes at the dry cleaners and notices that all of his clothes are shrinking, especially his trousers. He doesn't complain; he just goes out and buys trousers in a larger size. Tony is in the oblivious stage.

Tony quickly realizes that it is going to be expensive to replace his entire wardrobe. He thinks, my body has changed, and my usual amount of exercise and diet is not keeping my weight down. Tony has moved into the contemplation stage. This is the time when you take a step back and ask yourself: What do I really need to do to change?

Tony wants to do something about his weight "issue," but the holidays are upon him, and he does love eggnog and his wife's Christmas cookies. He is in no hurry to change. He spends the week between Christmas and New Year's readying himself to improve: He sets weight goals and determines a strategy for cutting back on calories and exercising more. His initial goal is to fit into his Marine uniform, but after trying it on, popping buttons like the Incredible Hulk (much to the entertainment of his wife and kids), he readjusts his goal to losing ten pounds. Realistic goals are important.

From the preparation state, Tony moves to action. In January, on his first business trip to Arizona, Tony packs running shoes. He makes sure to hit the fitness room at the hotel every morning and cuts back on night snacks and dark beer.

Tony hits his goal weight in August. He has lost the ten pounds and feels great. He adopts a new lifestyle, but then autumn comes and with that Oktoberfest beer. Since he is now at his ideal weight, Tony feels justified in ordering a dark beer. That one transgression becomes a few, and soon Tony is back in the oblivious mode.

It is difficult to change but even more challenging to sustain the change. In chapter 6 on accountability, we will discuss strategies to keep you on track.

Weight is an easy metric to quantify, and so is revenue performance as a salesperson. Are you a top, moderate, or underperformer? If you want to improve your performance, what are the necessary steps that need to be taken?

OBLIVIOUS IS NOT FUNNY, OR IS IT?

We love movies, and one of our favorites is *Young Frankenstein,* starring Gene Wilder and Marty Feldman. In this Mel Brooks comedy, Wilder plays Dr. Frankenstein's grandson, who has inherited the castle. He arrives to continue his grandfather's experiments and, in a wonderful scene, meets his grandfather's assistant, the hunchbacked Igor (Feldman). Being a physician of some note, Wilder offers to fix the hump on Igor's back. Igor replies, "What hump?"

THE MOST DEPRESSING DAY OF THE YEAR

A few years back a headline in *USA Today* read: "January 21st Most Depressing Day of the Year." According to the article, anti-depressant drug websites get the most hits on January 21, which is probably a good indication that it is a depressing day. The article went on to conjecture why that day of all days would be the most depressing. The top three theories? In third place was post-Christmas credit card bills arriving and putting people in a funk. In second place was the weather. January is a dreary month, with colder temperatures and shorter days. In first place was the belief that, by January 21, most people probably have given up on their New Year's resolution and were down in the dumps about it.

As we discussed in the five stages of change, people who set New Year's resolutions are usually stuck in the "contemplation" stage. The date of January 21st is also ironic when you consider the old saying that it takes twenty-one days to form or break a habit. People who are serious about change don't set New Year's resolutions. Instead, they research what it is really going to take to change. They develop a plan and execute it. Repeated action drives adoption of new behavior.

What It Takes to Be a Top Performer

When we look at top performers, we consider four things: skills, purpose, motivation, and behavior. To achieve top performance, you need to ask yourself some questions. See figure 3.

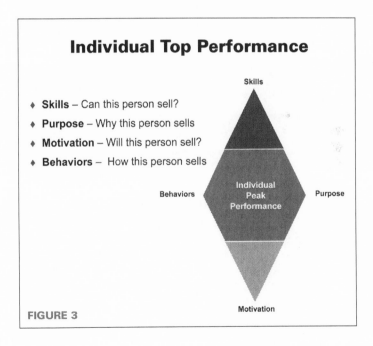

Individual Top Performance

- ♦ **Skills** – Can this person sell?
- ♦ **Purpose** – Why this person sells
- ♦ **Motivation** – Will this person sell?
- ♦ **Behaviors** – How this person sells

Skills

Behaviors

Individual Peak Performance

Purpose

Motivation

FIGURE 3

◆ **Skills:** Can you sell? In other words, do you have
the skill? We often ask clients if they know highly
skilled people who are not successful. Usually a
high number of hands go up. We once worked
with an individual who had an MBA from one of
the top business schools in the country and had
read every book on selling and account management. In fact, he could tell you what to do in every
situation. Still, quarter in and quarter out, he was
the worst performer on the team. Why? When we
needed to find him, all we had to do was call his
office because he was always in his office (instead
of meeting with customers)! Skills do not guarantee success or execution.

◆ **Purpose**: Why do you sell? Deep down, what is
your purpose? As we noted in the beginning, not
everyone wants to go into sales. But if you find
purpose in what you do, if you really love your job,
you will be more successful at it.

◆ **Motivation:** Will you sell? Do you have the desire
and initiative required to succeed? One manager
told us of his top performer, Aaron, who did not
have a high skill set but was extremely motivated.
In fact, if you walked into Aaron's office, you
would find a picture of the new boat he planned to
buy and the new truck that he would need to purchase to pull the boat. Aaron loved material things
that money bought, and it drove his behavior. "He
was my top guy consistently," the manager said.

"However, because he was so motivated with a lower skill set, he was like a bull in a china shop. I was always cleaning up after him. No one could stop him once he identified an opportunity, and he would see whoever he needed to get the deal done. I would rather have someone motivated and clean up after him when he made his numbers, rather than listen to excuses why someone didn't make his quota."

◆ **Behavior:** How do you sell? Are your actions in alignment with your goals and objectives? We know a salesperson who routinely says, "Not so fast," even though the senior executive decision maker is ready to buy his service. "I want to make sure there is a good business fit," says Jack, the salesperson. "Let's schedule a time to review my recommendation, and in the meantime, let me talk to members of your team to learn more about your business. If I feel a good fit exists after that, we can do business." Keep in mind, the executive was ready to buy now! However, Jack's selling process is so disciplined, he knows that there are certain things he needs to do to be successful. Ironically, when it is time to meet with the executive again, Jack presents a larger, more encompassing solution based on his research. It *is* a better fit, and the executive ends ups signing a bigger contract than he would have originally. Most salespeople think this top performer is slowing the process down, when, in fact, he is ensuring a high close ratio while developing a network of people who will want to work with him again and again.

Developing Self-Awareness

Accurate self-assessment means knowing one's inner resources, abilities, and limits. In his book *Working with Emotional Intelligence,* Daniel Goleman describes people with this competency (self-awareness):

- Aware of their strengths and weaknesses.

- Reflective and able to learn from experience.

- Open to candid feedback, new perspectives, continuous learning, and self-development.

Self-awareness is what distinguishes man from animals, according to German psychoanalyst Erich Fromm. "[Man] knew that he existed and that he was something different, something apart from nature, apart from other people, too," Fromm wrote. "He experienced himself. He was aware that he thought and felt. As far as we know, there is nothing analogous to this anywhere in the animal kingdom. That is the specific quality that makes human beings human."

Self-awareness is also the quality that makes top performers who they are. Without self-awareness, we are like Igor, running around the castle, unable to improve our lot in life.

We have worked with hundreds of salespeople to improve their self-awareness and have developed some strategies to help you.

◆ **Pay attention.** Pay closer attention to your past sales results. Do not be too quick to dismiss past failures as being outside your control or influence. That doesn't mean you should obsess over them. Just see what you can learn from them.

◆ **Seek out feedback.** Seek out those who work closely with you and get their input on everything—from your skills and competencies to attitudes and behaviors. Create your own board of advisors. Go into this with an open mind. Leave your ego at the door. When you ask for someone's opinion, be ready to accept it.

◆ **Benchmark others.** Compare yourself to others whose attributes and/or skills you admire. We all have heroes, people we want to be like. Maybe it's a famous person, your dad or your mom, or the guy at the next desk. Some coaches tell their players not to look at personal game film, but to study the films of the greats in their sport, if they want to improve. A young basketball player who compares his game to Michael Jordan's will quickly become aware of his strengths and weaknesses.

◆ **Utilize assessment tools.** Gain a more accurate picture of yourself through assessment tools. While no assessment tool is 100 percent accurate, they can provide additional input, give you food for thought, and point you to areas that need development.

A study at Cornell University found that when it comes to self-assessment, 75 percent of salespeople believe they are above average. Men typically inflate their assessment, while women are harder on themselves. So many of us don't have an accurate picture of who we really are and how we perform. That's why it is important to use all of these strategies, in concert, to improve self-awareness and become the top performer in your team.

REFLECTION EXERCISES

What are my greatest strengths as a contributor to my company?

What are my greatest limitations as a contributor to my company?

What would my severest critics say about me—even if I don't agree?

CHAPTER 4

HAVING THE RIGHT ATTITUDE

"Attitude is a little thing that makes a big difference."

**WINSTON CHURCHILL,
POLITICIAN AND STATESMAN**

IN SALES, YOU ARE SUBJECTED TO MORE UPS and downs than in any other profession. Average performers experience more rejection than acceptance. Think about all of the areas of selling that your attitude impacts:

- ◆ **Elevating contact level:** Do you feel worthy of contacting executive-level decision makers? Are you confident that you can bring them value?

- ◆ **Handling detractors:** When a contact looks you in the eye and says, "Everything goes through me," do you buckle? Or do you recognize that sometimes your attitude needs to be that "no one person can control my actions at this account"?

◆ **Seeing the value in your own product:** If you don't believe in your own gut that your product is worth more, then that attitude is going to be projected in everything you say and do.

Your attitude is how you respond, positively or negatively, toward a certain idea, object, person, or situation. It is closely related to your opinions and beliefs, and it is based upon your experiences. An important point to remember: learning oftentimes involves changing your attitude.

In chapter 2, we talked about the account managers who didn't want to learn presentation skills. Most of them came from an operational background (versus a sales background), and the idea of standing in front of their customer executives and giving a formal presentation of the data scared them to death. They wanted to stay in their comfort zone, which was sitting down and reviewing the data with their customers, perhaps over a cup of coffee. These account managers had an "opinion" about presenting, which was that it wasn't part of their job. They had a "belief" that their customers did not want to be presented to. And, this belief was based on some uncomfortable "experiences" they had presenting in the past. To change their attitude, we had to show them the value of presenting. Once attitudes changed, they were able to learn presentation skills.

In short, you will not learn unless you have the right attitude.

What Makes a Successful Attitude?

Some might say that attitude is the most important attribute of top performers. It will help you climb that mountain of success more than any other attribute (motivation, accountability, and integrity). The right attitude is like good hiking boots; it will get you to the top and make the climb enjoyable, but you have to maintain it, checking it for wear and tear. Having a poor or negative attitude is like making that trek with old and inadequate hiking boots. Such an attitude drags you down; makes the work hard, if not impossible; leaves you tired and broken; and doesn't get you to your goal.

There are three aspects of attitude when it comes to top performers: optimism, self-confidence, and willingness to step out of your comfort zone. We will go into these in more detail later in this chapter, but here are a few brief notes:

◆ **Optimism:** Psychologist Martin Seligman spent years studying the relationship between positive thinking and sales success. He developed an optimism test that was given to a large group of Metropolitan Life Insurance Company salespeople. When scores were matched to actual sales records, it turned out that agents who scored in the top half for optimism sold 37 percent more insurance over two years than those in the more pessimistic bottom half. More notable still, agents who scored in the top 10 percent for optimism sold 88 percent more than those ranked in the most pessimistic 10 percent.

- **Self-confidence:** Legendary coach Vince Lombardi led the Green Bay Packers to five NFL championships and two Super Bowl victories. He stressed winning all the time, even in preseason games, because it instilled self-confidence in his players. He believed confidence could make "winners of losers" and suggested that anyone can "get in the habit of winning" and develop a "winning expectation" by setting simple, small goals and doing one's best.

- **Willingness to step out of your comfort zone:** Top performers are willing to stretch their comfort zones. They try new things, go the extra mile, and take chances—and often they succeed just because they were willing to try. With each success, their comfort zone grows bigger, which means now they can reach even farther.

 TIP *The bigger the risks you take, the bigger the rewards. Your self-confidence tends to grow in direct proportion to the risks you take. The goal is to succeed when you take risks, but success is not required if you can reflect and learn from what did not work.*

A Negative Attitude Has a Far-reaching Impact

Viewing your "glass as half empty" will have an impact on your sales performance and so much more. The effects of negativity include:

- **Depression:** Depression disorders affect approximately 18.8 million American adults or about 9.5 percent of the US population age eighteen and older in a given year. Depression coupled with the wrong attitude can be dangerous.

◆ **Lower productivity at work:** When you are in a bad mood or a low state of mind, do you feel motivated to get your work done? Or do you mentally "check out"? When you are upbeat and positive, you are naturally in a more productive state of mind.

◆ **Physical health:** Ever notice how a stressful time is often followed by illness—a cold or the flu? Many studies have proven the connection between mental and emotional stress and the effect it has in lowering the immune system.

◆ **Overreacting to life's challenges:** Stuff happens. Sometimes we deal with it with grace and patience, and sometimes we overreact. A good example is being at the airport and learning that your flight has been delayed due to inclement weather or mechanical problems. We've all been there. If we are emotionally adjusted, we recognize there is nothing we can do about it, open up our laptop, and get some work done. Unfortunately, not everyone at the gate is that emotionally well-adjusted. There is almost always one person standing at the counter yelling at the gate agent about a situation in which the agent has no control. It does not improve the situation. It does nothing but raise the customer's blood pressure, the agent's stress level, and everyone else's discomfort level.

◆ **Enjoyment of life:** In his best-selling book *Learned Optimism,* Seligman sums up the impact of being negative. He said that, in all his years of research, he found that negative people get sick more often, are divorced more frequently, raise kids who get in more trouble, and earn less money. This reminds us of that classic scene from the Bill Murray movie *Stripes* where he has just had his car repossessed, been fired from his job, and lost his girlfriend. He then turns to the camera and dead-pans, "And then, depression set in."

What Stands Between You and the Right Attitude?

Over time, continued exposure to the wrong influences can seriously affect our levels of optimism. We are not saying you get to blame your poor or dipping sales performance on these obstacles. This section is not a get-out-of-jail-free card. It is a discussion, however, of what sometimes builds barriers to having the right attitude. If you want to be a top performer, it is your job to find a way around, over, under, or through these obstacles:

◆ **Weak support system:** Pessimism can be contagious. Do you have the right people in your support system? Mahatma Gandhi once said, "I will not let anyone walk through my mind with their dirty feet." We all enjoy being around positive people more than sad sacks, but now researchers have proven that being around negative people can make us more negative as well. It is human nature to mirror the mood of the person you are talking to. The longer you talk to them, the more likely you are to take on their mood. Have you ever had dinner with a friend who does nothing but find fault with her life and the world in general, and when you exited the restaurant, you felt worse than when you entered—down, out of sorts, and tired? Limit your exposure to pessimistic people, for your own good.

◆ **Upbringing:** "The fruit doesn't fall far from the tree" is an old saying, but there is really no proof of a genetic connection when it comes to negativity. Negative parents may raise negative children simply because, as in the prior point, prolonged exposure to negative people can turn you into one of them. A senior executive at a large insurance company had an interesting reaction to his success and the riches that followed—guilt! As he reflected, a lot of his guilt was a result of his upbringing. While he was growing up, his parents instilled in him a value system that actually looked down on people who strived for material or financial success. He realized that this attitude toward success was a huge barrier that he needed to overcome in order to take his performance to the next level.

◆ **No purpose:** Having purpose is essential to a successful sales career. Few aimless people climb the ranks. We said that great salespeople may have fallen into their careers but eventually the careers got into them. When you lack purpose in your career, it becomes more difficult to get out of bed each morning full of positive energy to get things done.

◆ **No spirituality:** A sense of spirituality can play a key role in keeping negativity in perspective and preventing it from consuming you. Some people find spirituality in religion, while others find it volunteering or giving back to the community, taking long nature walks, and getting in touch with the essence of who they are. No matter how you define spirituality, it is important because it helps you put life's setbacks in the proper perspective.

◆ **It's biological:** Why are some people more optimistic than others? It turns out that it can be biology at work. Seligman describes this well in *Learned Optimism*: "What keeps us moving toward our goals comes down to the prefrontal brain circuit's ability to remind us of how satisfied we will feel when we accomplish those goals. The left prefrontal brain circuits do us another favor: they quiet the feelings of frustration or worry that might discourage us from continuing the pursuit of our goals." Pessimistic people can become consumed by their negative feelings. It is proven that an attitude of defeat or panic can be debilitating and shut down the central nervous system. Conversely, an attitude of confidence or determination releases something you experience during a good workout—endorphins.

Self-Talk: What Are You Talking Yourself Into?

Another possible barrier to having the right attitude is the way we talk to ourselves. People who give up easily believe that the bad things that happen to them are permanent. They believe they can't win and that everything is out of their control. They're the people who have this internal dialogue: "Not this again. I can never catch a break."

People with this attitude talk themselves into failure. They tell themselves: "My quota is always unrealistic" or "All the customer cares about is price." After awhile, it becomes so ingrained that it changes how they perform in selling situations (leading with price all the time instead of finding out what is really important to the customer).

Research shows that when we aren't reading a book or consuming other media, we are having a conversation with ourselves that can be as high as four hundred words per minute. The question is what is the tone and content of that conversation? Pessimists tend to make universal or general statements such as "Our prices are always higher." Optimists, on the other hand, are able to isolate a negative situation, view it as far from permanent, and express themselves in more specific terms such as "One of our products, the System 180, is 20 percent higher than the competition's."

Nothing—good or bad—lasts forever. It only seems that way sometimes. A negative situation can change with a single thought.

JUST FAN-TAS-TIC

How we react to life's setbacks often defines the type of person we are. We have a good friend who has started and sold many businesses. He told us the most important ingredient to being a successful entrepreneur is dealing with life's setbacks. He said, "When something bad happens to me or one of my businesses, I say out loud, 'That's just fan-tas-tic! Something good will come from this.'" Of course, he doesn't stand around waiting for the windfall. He proactively and enthusiastically figures out how to turn the situation around, but he starts with the right attitude.

It is the way he runs his businesses and the way he approaches life. For example, just days after buying a new, top-of-the-line Mercedes Benz, he took his wife to a Minnesota Vikings preseason football game. When they decided to leave the game early, the valet had trouble finding his car. He turned to his wife and said, "My car has been stolen."

Sure enough, after nearly ten minutes of searching, the valet returned and began to apologize profusely, "Sir, I am sorry, but it appears your Mercedes has been stolen."

Expecting a meltdown, the valet was shocked when our friend said, "That's just fan-tas-tic! You know, I really wanted a different color, but they didn't have it in stock at the time. Plus, I have been paying a lot of money in car insurance over the years; it's about time I get payback from my insurance company. Why don't you contact the police and call me a cab, and we'll get out of your hair?" The valet walked away in a daze.

This new twist on the old "when life deals you lem-ons . . ." is fan-tas-tic.

An Additional Note: Having a sense of humor helps. Chip recently told the "Just Fan-tas-tic" story to a group of clients. A few days later, he received an e-mail from the sales executive that went something like this:

"Hey, Chip, half my team and I are stuck in the Balti-more airport due to the tornadoes in Alabama—and that's just fantastic! We have been able to spend these many hours getting to know each other better. We are even thinking of getting matching tattoos as we wait for a flight out of here!"

OPTIMISM

Give Yourself an Attitude Adjustment

Top performers are optimistic. We aren't born with opti-mism; it is not genetic. It is a disposition, a way of viewing the world, that can be developed. There are many ways to proactively adjust your attitude. We break them into three categories: mental, physical, and spiritual adjust-ments (figure 4).

Mental Attitude Adjustments

Mental attitude adjustments focus on using your thought process to improve your attitude. Here are some strategies:

Do a self-assessment. It is important for us all to peri-odically step back and ask, "What impacts my attitude positively and negatively? What is standing in the way of

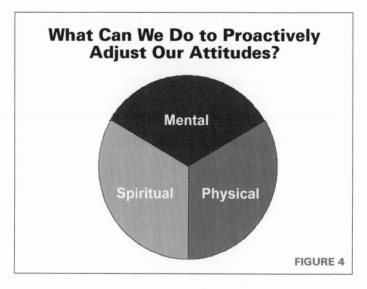

What Can We Do to Proactively Adjust Our Attitudes?

Mental

Spiritual   Physical

FIGURE 4

me and a better attitude?" (Go back and look at the Reflection Exercise at the end of chapter 3.)

Employ positive self-talk. According to Dr. Martin Seligman (in the book *Learned Optimism*), successful people think twice as many positive thoughts as negative people. So talk positively to yourself! It might feel funny doing it, but maybe it wouldn't hurt if we were all a little more like Stuart Smalley on *Saturday Night Live*: "I like myself; I like myself; I'm good enough; and, dang it, people like me." Positive self-talk reprograms us to expect success. We envision ourselves succeeding in a big sales pitch and employ the inner dialogue to support that vision. Athletes do this all the time to prepare themselves to play at peak performance; why wouldn't we do the same thing?

Change your circumstances. Think for a moment about the type of media that you consume. Al, a salesman who travels a lot, discovered that one of the things that was impacting his attitude the most was the way he was spending his "windshield time" between customer meetings. He listened to talk radio. Well, what is the nature of talk radio? People duking it out over controversial topics. Can you imagine listening to people argue all day long, getting out of your car, and being in the right frame of mind to see your customers? Not long after taking one of our workshops, Al e-mailed us that now he listens to comedy CDs in the car, and it has made a difference to his energy and sales performance.

In another example, Sally told us she plays her favorite songs while driving in the car to get her in the right frame of mind before a big presentation. She admits one song that really pumps her up is Rick Springfield's "Jessie's Girl," which brings back memories of her husband dancing to that very song. If something is bringing you down, change it. Choose inspiring music or CDs by motivational speakers such as Brian Tracy, Dennis Waitley, and Zig Ziglar.

Celebrate incremental success. If you are in sales or account management, you are rewarded (and punished) for success through the attainment (or lack of attainment) of your sales or retention goals. A great quarter or year can go a long way toward keeping you positive, but how do you handle an off-quarter or even an off-year? It is at these critical times that we need to reward ourselves for the effort we are putting in and focus on our leading indicators of success. Get into the habit of rewarding yourself for incremental improvement. When you reach a personal goal, give yourself a pat on the back: get tickets for a special event (a ballgame or a Broadway show), buy a new business suit or the latest fly fishing gear you've been eyeing, or take a trip with the family. One salesman put together an aggressive activity-based plan that included driving more prospecting calls each week, making more new business presentations each month, and generating more proposals each quarter. When he accomplished this goal (whether he was at his sales goal or not), he was going to reward himself with a new set of golf clubs. This is the attitude a resilient salesperson needs to have, especially in a down or recovering economy.

Speak positively about others. Have you ever gone to lunch with some coworkers and all they do is bash the poor souls who aren't there? Does it make you wonder what they are saying about you when you aren't around? Try changing the tone of those lunch conversations entirely. Start speaking positively about others when they aren't around. Not only will you feel better about yourself, but you will find more people wanting to be around you.

Make your job a career. "Choose a job you love, and you will never have to work a day in your life," according to Confucius. Think of your purpose as the rudder that guides you through your career. If that rudder is broken or not set deep enough, you can go off course. As we said in the introduction of this book, top performers may have fallen into their careers, but at some point their career got into them. Their rudder is strong and set deep, and there is no doubt that has a positive impact on attitude. (We will dig deeper into the purpose behind what we do for a living and why we do it in chapter 5 on motivation.)

Physical Attitude Adjustments

Taking care of ourselves physically can have a dramatic effect on our attitude. Consider some of these strategies for physical attitude adjustments:

Manage your energy. In the best-selling book *Power of Full Engagement,* Tony Schwartz and Jim Loehr profess that most businesspeople today have a bigger problem than time management, and that is "energy management." The authors spent years researching the top athletes in the world and discovered that what differentiated the top athletes was their "system for recovery." One of the athletes they researched was golfer Jack Nicklaus. They observed how Jack was extremely focused right before and during his tee shot. Then as he walked down the fairway, he would relax and talk to his caddie or playing partner about anything under the sun (accept his next shot). It wasn't until he was approaching his ball that he would begin to really focus on his distance, the wind, and other critical variables that would shape how he approached the upcoming shot. When the researchers asked him why he did this, Nicklaus said that if all he did between shots was obsess about the next shot, for eighteen holes, four days in a row, he would be mentally exhausted. This is what is meant by having a system for recovery.

What is your system? We are fans of the executive power nap (EPN). Unless you have mastered the art of the power nap, you will not appreciate its value. Here's how it works: Sneak away for ten or fifteen minutes and put your head down on your desk, or recline the seat in your car and close your eyes for a brief time. Just as you begin to get to the point of being unconscious, end the nap. Research has shown that you will get more benefit from a short nap than a long one. In fact, taking an hour-long nap can actually cause you to be drowsy the remainder of the day. A nap isn't the only way to recover between meetings and sales calls. What relaxes you and fills you with energy? Singing, playing guitar, juggling, taking a walk around the block? Find out what helps you recover and make it part of your life.

Exercise. People who exercise regularly report having more energy at work and throughout the course of the day. When you feel energized, your attitude rises. Choose an exercise that you enjoy and works with your lifestyle. If you want to start a running program, there are many books, websites, and apps to help you develop a fitness plan and take it on the running trail. If you have bad feet, cranky knees, or just don't like running, consider walking, biking, or swimming. Swimming provides a fantastic cardiovascular workout, and it's easy on the joints. If you are a "road warrior," make sure you can maintain your exercise routine on your business trips. Throwing a pair of running shoes and swim or workout gear into your suitcase is easy; nearly all hotels have fitness rooms, treadmills, or pools.

TIP *View work as a series of short sprints. In their book, Schwartz and Loehr advocate viewing work (and life) as a series of short sprints instead of a marathon. When you take on this attitude, you naturally recognize the need to take a breather in between sprints, while marathoners keep going and going until they are exhausted.*

Improve your sleeping habits. Sleep researchers maintain that happy people get at least eight hours of sleep each night. That's easy for the scientists to say. Getting quality sleep can be challenging. All kinds of things keep us awake: sick children, financial worries, creative problems, work concerns. Here's an idea for improving the quality of your sleep time: Once clocking eight hours of sleep was no problem for Amy, a top sales performer, but Amy has noticed that as she gets older, she often sleeps hard for three or four hours and then wakes up, alert, and spends the rest of the night wide awake. She lies in bed trying to get back to sleep. Her mind races over all of the things she needs to get done the next day, or she starts worrying about an account, a customer, or a problem with a coworker. She tries getting up and watching television, but that just makes her even more awake. After much experimentation, Amy found a solution that works for her. When she can't sleep, she doesn't fight it anymore. Instead, she simply gets up, grabs a book, and heads to the living room for thirty or forty minutes of good reading. Reading settles her mind and lulls her back into a drowsy state. Amy supplements this solution with an executive power nap. On nights when she only gets five or six hours of sleep, Amy makes sure she takes an EPN around 3:00

or 4:00 p.m. It does wonders to re-energize Amy and keep her in top form for meeting the needs of her customers.

Eat right and drink right. We admit we like junk food, chocolate, and French fries. That's why we exercise; so we can indulge in the occasional unhealthy temptation. We are not nutritionists and are not here to tell you what to eat or not eat. However, we do encourage you to learn how your body reacts to certain foods and drinks and make sure you eat right and drink right before an important client meeting or new business presentation. Let's look at Matt. He likes a few beers as much as the next guy. But as he has gotten older, he has found that having a few drinks the night before a big presentation reduces his sharpness the next day. This impacts his performance and the company's bottom line. Are those few beers really worth it?

Sales managers tell us in our sales training that dealing with a salesperson with a drinking problem is one of the toughest issues. They see these individuals overdoing it at a client conference or at a national sales meeting and can't help but wonder how they are representing the company when they are back in their territories. There is a fine line between being a social drinker and being an alcoholic. Key questions to ask yourself: How does my drinking affect my performance at work? And how does my drinking affect my personal life? If you don't like the sound of either of these questions, it may be time to do something about it.

Give yourself a new look. Fernando Lamas (Billy Crystal) on *Saturday Night Live* used to say, "It is better to look good than to feel good, darling." Well, we think these two are actually tied together because often times we feel good when we look good. As a sales professional, you must invest in your looks because first impressions are critical and because clients who see you on a regular basis are keeping track of how you look. Even if you don't have an endless budget for clothes, choose quality over quantity. We talked earlier about rewarding ourselves for incremental success, this could be a great way to reward yourself. Set a stringent activity-based goal, and when you achieve it, reward yourself with an expensive pair of shoes or a suit that you wouldn't normally buy. Or a Hartmann briefcase or Tumi backpack.

Don't let age consume you. We are an aging population that is likely going to need to work to an older age than our parents did. So staying in shape is important. Are you obsessed with growing older? Do you complain incessantly about your aches and pains? Then remember, age is just a number. Look at Jack LaLanne, the "godfather of fitness." He brought fitness into the lives of millions of Americans with his fitness television show, which aired from 1951 to 1985. Every year, LaLanne celebrated his birthday by accomplishing an incredible physical feat. He celebrated his eightieth birthday the way few others could—by swimming 1.5 miles shackled to and towing eighty boats with eighty people from the Queensway Bay Bridge in the Long Beach Harbor to the Queen Mary. This is a stretch of water with high winds and currents. Unbelievable! To Jack LaLanne, age was truly just a number.

KNOW WHAT YOU'RE DRINKING

Steve thought he was making a wise choice when he limited himself to one diet drink a day, at lunch. Then Lent rolled around and his children asked what his Lenten resolution was. Because he couldn't think of anything on the spur of the moment, he said, "I'm giving up my diet drink." After several weeks without his diet drink at lunch, Steve began to notice some differences in the way he felt in the afternoon. He would typically get drowsy around 2:00 or 3:00 p.m. This wasn't happening anymore! He discovered that coming down off of the caffeine high from the diet drink was really lowering his energy level. Without the drink, his energy levels stayed more consistent throughout the day.

This is not a story about whether or not you should drink diet soda. It is about being aware of what foods and drinks do to you: Do they energize you? Do they make you feel sluggish? Do they bring you up only to send you crashing down? Investigate how you can put together a nutrition plan that will help you become a top and consistent performer.

Spiritual Attitude Adjustments

We've talked about a number of strategies for improving attitude by making mental and physical adjustments. It is now time to discuss something a bit deeper and sometimes more complex to adjust: our spirituality.

Here are some strategies to help you put things in the proper perspective and affect your attitude positively:

Believe you are part of something bigger. People become stressed out about situations in life that often really aren't worth stressing about. As the saying goes, "Don't sweat the small stuff, and it's all small stuff!" Have you ever stressed about something and then months later asked yourself, "Why did I let THAT stress me?" Successful people are able to put life's setbacks in the proper perspective. The next time you experience a tongue lashing from the boss, or a loud complaint from a key customer, step away and say: "This won't get me down" or "The sun will still come up tomorrow" or "I'm healthy, my kids are healthy, and that is what is really important."

Develop a sense of purpose. Attitude is connected to a sense of purpose. Purpose gets to the essence of knowing why you are doing what you are doing with your life. As we discussed earlier, many of us may have fallen into a sales career, but people who are successful eventually develop a purpose for what they are doing. That purpose may revolve around a sense of duty to look out for your customer's best interests, or a commitment to providing for your spouse and kids, or even a sense of obligation to do well for your manager and your company. Whatever you determine to be your purpose, having one can help you to mitigate the setbacks you experience on any given day. (We will talk more about purpose in chapter 5 on motivation.)

Encourage and help others. Many of us know the great value we can provide to others by volunteering to coach or mentor. What we may not realize is that it's a two-way street: we receive great value when we mentor. Think about how good you feel when someone asks for your guidance or is able to implement something you have suggested. Spirituality may be as simple as volunteering at a soup kitchen, coaching youth sports, or participating in a mentoring program. Spirituality is about being of service to others.

Know what you want out of life. Many people stumble through life never thinking long and hard about what they really want out of life. NFL head coach Dennis Green's mantra was "Faith, family, and football." His advice illustrated not only the value of setting priorities in one's life, but setting the *right* priorities. For Green, the third focus, football, would not be possible without the first two: faith and family. Not sure what you want? Here's a quick little exercise: Write your eulogy, right here and right now. Visualize what you need to do to have a happy, well-adjusted, and fulfilling life—like the one you described in your eulogy.

OWN YOUR JOB—NO MATTER WHAT IT IS

A great example of knowing what you want out of life is Mark, a maintenance worker at a health club Scott frequents. Mark is the person who cleans the locker room, sauna, toilets, and equipment. Scott has quietly observed Mark as he interacts with all the members. He is always energized, upbeat, and working hard. He has made it a point to learn as many members' names as he can. How often do you find someone that committed to their job? Unknowing members could look upon Mark and say, he is just a janitor at a health club, but to Mark, he sees his job as much more important than that. He believes he is building relationships that will affect the loyalty of the members and, guess what, he's right! Many members have acknowledged to Scott that Mark *is* the health club and the reason they continue to patronize that specific club.

Mark is truly a peak performer (whether his employers recognize it or not). He takes pride in a job well done and is committed to results. There was an old Mac McAnally song that Jimmy Buffett sang called "It's My Job." The song asks a street sweeper why he whistles and is so happy while he labors on the street, and he says, "It's my job to be cleaning up this mess and that's enough reason to go for me . . ." That's right, it's your job! Own it. Make it interesting.

> *"The key question to keep asking is:*
> *Are you spending your time on the right things?*
> *Because time is all you have. "*
> RANDY PAUSCH, THE LAST LECTURE

SELF-CONFIDENCE

Self-Confidence Gives You an Edge in Selling

Self-confidence is essential for success in sales. We are not talking about the brash confidence that says, "I can sell anything to anybody, even if they don't need it or want it." We are talking about that quiet, inner confidence that knows you can handle some of the many tough situations a person in sales encounters: meeting with and persuading senior-level customers, presenting new solutions, and dealing with detractors to your company and product.

Self-confidence is the expected probability that a person will achieve a goal in a certain situation. Here are some facts about self-confidence:

It is situational, not absolute. Some people have a lot of self-confidence in one area of their life but less confidence in others. It is a rare person who is confident he or she can handle *anything*. Aren't there some situations that you seem to breeze through, while others that set you trembling in fear? (See "Bet You Can't Make It" in this chapter.)

It is a good predictor of performance. Just look at sports. Over and over, we see our favorite athletes play brilliantly when they are confident. But what happens on the days when they don't believe in themselves? They are unable to make a basket, connect with the ball, or score the goal. In 1999, Chip had the opportunity to see his basketball idol, Michael Jordan, play in person for the first time. This was Jordan's last year as a Chicago Bull, and he was nearing the end of his career. In this particular game, Jordan was horrible; he missed a lot of easy shots, including a dunk. Chip couldn't help but think that he had waited way too long to see his idol play in person. At least it was a close game, which made it worthwhile. Interesting enough, at the end of the game with the score tied and the Bulls calling a play in the huddle, it was a no-brainer as to whose number was being called. Everyone in that arena, every Bulls player, and Jordan himself knew who was going to take the last shot, even though Jordan had shot poorly all game. Now that is confidence!

It is tied to self-fulfilling prophesies. If you don't believe you can do a job, then you won't be able to do it. Top performers speak and act with confidence. "I can . . ." and "I will . . ." create a self-fulfilling prophecy.

BET YOU CAN'T MAKE IT

Every year, we take a golf trip with a group of high school buddies. This is a group of guys that no one in high school pegged for success. In fact, if you had asked our high school teachers if we would turn out to be successful in life, the answer would have come back an emphatic no! However, each one of us has been extremely successful in our own right; we've started and are running our own businesses.

Our golf trip is always competitive because that is the kind of people we are: successful entrepreneurs used to taking risks. We want to win just for the sake of it but also because we bet on the outcome. It has been interesting to watch, over the years, how the pressure of playing for money affects composure, even in senior business leaders who make big decisions daily in the boardroom. Different venue, different situation. When the game comes down to it and there's money on the line, anyone can blow a three-foot putt.

It's happened to us, and it's happened to our buddies. Still, we learn from these experiences and from the pressure. And we take what we learn—how we handled it, how we survived it—to build a self-confidence that we can use on the golf course and on the job. The more challenges you take on, the easier they become.

Barriers to Self-Confidence in Selling

What are some of the obstacles that can affect self-confidence and your success as a salesperson?

- **Low self-concept:** Self-concept is defined as your opinion of yourself. If you have a low opinion of yourself, you have a tremendous barrier to developing confidence in anything, let alone getting access to a key senior-level executive. This relates directly back to your attitude. What is your attitude about yourself? A self-concept that is too low or too high (as is the case with some salespeople) can stand in the way of your success. If you don't think you belong, you don't. Psychologist David McClelland said self-esteem is the number one denominator that drives success.

- **Past failures:** Past failures are like ghosts; they haunt us, if we let them. Much of our self-confidence is shaped around our experiences and how we handled them. If we did not do well, it could give our self-confidence a serious slap. Consider how you look at past failures. Do you dwell on them or do you shake them off and set your sights on new territory?

- **Lack of preparation:** Most of the top athletes are peak performers because they prepared themselves to win. They put in the time and effort in the weight room, on the running track, and on the playing field to build their self-confidence and consistently practice their trade. Michael Jordan, arguably one of the best basketball players ever, was known to be the first one in the gym and the last to leave. Practice is boring, and that is why most salespeople don't do it. However, if you are not getting the results you want, it may be your lack of preparation. We suggest salespeople role play to learn how to successfully position their product and company and how to conduct and close the sales call. Role play your prospecting script. Rehearse your presentations and get feedback from peers. Be the first one in the office and the last to leave until you are getting the results you want. Incidentally, Michael Jordan worked hard regardless of how successful he was because he wanted to compete at the highest level—and so should you.

◆ **Lack of knowledge:** With the vast amount of information available on selling, this should never be an issue. However, it is important to understand your learning style. What is your best way to learn how to be a better salesperson? Do you grasp concepts easily from books and articles and can quickly put them into practice in your career? Or do you absorb information better through training and one-on-one mentoring? While knowledge is power, applying knowledge is what's truly important. Amazingly, some low performers have never taken the time to understand their products, the industry they are selling to, and their customer's business.

◆ **Unrealistic expectations:** Set realistic expectations and goals. Incremental successes build self-confidence. Plus, all those small successes eventually accrue into big successes as your self-confidence grows.

◆ **No belief:** Do you believe you can land that "impossible" account? Belief will take you a long way. In 1980, a "miracle" happened on the ice at the Winter Olympics in Lake Placid, New York. A group of American youngsters pulled a historic upset, beating out a team of highly skilled and highly favored hockey champions from the Soviet Union. The kids didn't believe they could do it, but famed coach Herb Brooks did and, eventually, he convinced them as well. Sometimes, the only thing that stands between victory and defeat is the belief that you *can* do it.

FROM COACH HERB BROOKS'S "MIRACLE" SPEECH

"Great moments are born from great opportunity. And that's what you have here tonight, boys. That's what you've earned here tonight. One game. If we played 'em ten times, they might win nine. But not this game. Not tonight. Tonight, we skate with them. Tonight, we stay with them. And we shut them down because we can! Tonight, WE are the greatest hockey team in the world. . . . This is your time. Now go out there and take it."

Source: From the movie *Miracle on Ice,* http://www.imdb.com.

Strategies for Developing Self-Confidence

We all can't have a coach like Herb Brooks in our corner, giving a boost when we doubt ourselves. So how do we overcome self-doubt? The first step is to look at the barriers to self-confidence that we've just discussed and consider which might apply to you. Be honest with yourself. Once you know your obstacles, develop a plan to overcome them. Here are some useful strategies:

◆ **Model those you respect.** Identify people who have great confidence in the task you aspire to and model their behavior. Ask the top salespeople how they do it. Ask them where their confidence comes from. The authors of this book have modeled their speaking after Hall of Fame speaker Dr. Alan Zimmerman. Zimmerman always appeared to be a naturally gifted speaker able to tell stories with emotion and keep his audience on the edge of their seats. Early on in his career doing some intern work for Zimmerman, Chip came across some three-by-five cards created by Zimmerman for his speeches. Chip was amazed to see that every word of Zimmerman's speeches (right down to what sounded like ad lib stories) was written down word for word. In Chip's mind, Zimmerman went from being a naturally blessed speaker to someone who had worked incredibly hard to become a great speaker. It also served as a model to Chip and Scott as to what it takes to become a top performer.

◆ **Look for opportunities and take risks.** Nothing ventured, nothing gained. If you lack confidence at speaking in front of groups, volunteer to deliver a presentation at the next staff meeting. Raise your hand. Look for any opportunities to practice. It will force you to prepare, which is one big reason people lack confidence in a situation—they aren't ready for it. You will continue to get better with repetition; you will find out what works for you and what doesn't.

◆ **Commit to required action.** Make a real commitment to do the things you need to do to get better: role play sales calls, rehearse presentations, study successful salespeople. Just don't sit there and wish for more self-confidence. Take steps to build your confidence.

◆ **Practice, practice, practice.** Confident people seem to breeze through life; they make everything look so easy. What we don't see is the hours of practice they put into their craft. And don't kid yourself—selling is a craft. It can be mastered and honed to an art.

◆ **Avoid negative thought patterns.** It all comes back to your inner monologue. Is your self-talk negative or positive? Do you tell yourself: "I will never be a good speaker"? Or do you look into the mirror and say, "I'm hitting this presentation out of the park today"?

SOMETIMES YOU NEED TEAMMATES WHO PUSH YOU

Minnesota Viking great John Randle was recently inducted into the Pro Football Hall of Fame. In interviews leading up to his induction, he spoke about how his day-to-day battles in practice with offensive guard Randall McDaniel (another Hall of Famer) really pushed him to a level of high performance. Randle still remembers the day in practice (as do many other players) when he finally beat McDaniel. The point is: While some players go through the motion in practice, Randle and McDaniel practiced as if they were playing in a real game, thus preparing each other for top-level competition when game time actually came. They excelled because they prepared and practiced hard at all times.

COMFORT ZONE

Expand Your Comfort Zone for Top Performance

What is your comfort zone? It is a situation or place where you feel secure, comfortable, and in control. It's a nice place to be, but you really don't do any growing there. Top performers want to grow in their selling abilities, in their earning potential, and in their position in the company. They are willing to step out of their comfort zone. Staying in the same place is not acceptable to them. It's not any fun. It's not challenging.

Try to imagine what your comfort zone looks like. If you are a moderate performer or underachiever, your comfort zone is like a windowless room with one door.

You feel safe there, but you are limited. The only way in and out of the room is through the single door. Your potential for making more money and closing more deals is limited. You don't have a lot of options. You have to use the same door, the same methods, the same strategies.

Now look at the comfort zone of a top performer. This is a room that sort of resembles one of those restaurants on a tropical island. It has a roof, a floor, but no walls. The top performer can leave his comfort zone in many directions. The more directions he has, the more opportunities he has. His potential for great things—for landing that difficult but lucrative account, for making top salesperson of the year, for earning bonuses and commissions—keeps multiplying because his options continue to multiply. He has different choices; if one strategy doesn't work, he has the room to try another one.

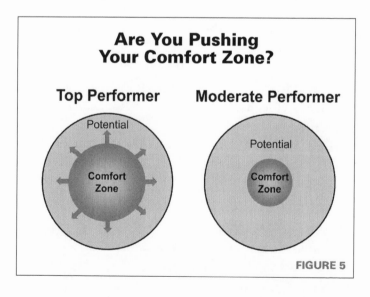

FIGURE 5

We often think of your comfort zone as a muscle. (See figure 5.) If you never exercise it or stretch it, it will atrophy, and you will never grow stronger. However, if you challenge that comfort zone, you will experience growth. You will be able to see far and go farther; your opportunities will expand. You will step out on the high wire of top performance and be confident.

PADDLING THROUGH RISK AND COMFORT ZONES

Dan Brattland is a character from our youth. He was a regular customer in the principal's office from the first grade on. Through the years, Dan continued to challenge the rules. "You're only going to live once" was his philosophy.

So what does this have to do with sales and top performance? Dan approached life by taking risks and challenging his comfort zones.

Dan has owned numerous businesses; some failed, while others he sold for a handsome profit. He is in it for the fun and racing heart as much as he's in it for the business. His zone is being outside his comfort level. He believes in himself and his ability to make everything happen. He is calloused to the risks and focuses on the rewards. Taking risks motivates Dan. On our annual golf trip, he still wants to be the one putting when all the money is riding.

Most importantly, through it all, he has always taken the time to savor the moment and enjoy the challenges and fruits of his labor.

When we decided to start our training company, we thought of friends like Dan. We both decided to leave good jobs (in which we were both partners) for an opportunity that was straight out of our comfort zones. We had no revenue, no client commitments, and a great idea that was not completely evolved. We also had supportive wives who stood behind us. It was the most liberating moment of our lives. We were confident in our abilities, although we knew failure was a possibility. That option of failure drove our actions.

Today, the risks we have taken define who we are and account for a significant portion of our self-confidence.

 TIP *The bigger the risks you take, the bigger the rewards. It is good to feel your heart beat in your chest—take that risk! If you are worried that you aren't "growing" your comfort zone, consider these tips:*

♦ *Start each day with the things you don't like to do but know you need to get done.*

♦ *The next time you feel reluctant to make a call, renew an acquaintance, or deliver a difficult message, catch yourself and recognize that this is a great opportunity to expand your comfort zone.*

♦ *Set a goal each month to expand your network of contacts or to elevate to higher levels within your accounts.*

"The greatest mistake a man can make is to be afraid of making one."

ELBERT HUBBARD, WRITER, PUBLISHER, ARTIST

Conclusion

Your attitude is not etched in stone. You can change it to become the top performer you want to be. You can have a winning attitude with optimism, self-confidence, and a willingness to step out of your comfort zone.

REFLECTION EXERCISES

When you don't have an optimistic attitude, how does that impact:

❖ Your performance at work?

❖ Your personal life?

❖ Your perception of your job?

List one thing you can do to impact your attitude:

❖ Mentally?

❖ Physically?

❖ Spiritually?

REFLECTION EXERCISES

Identify one task, situation or experience where you are not self-confident and answer the following:

❖ How does this affect your performance at work?

❖ Come up with two things you have learned in this chapter that you can apply to increase your confidence.

❖ When was the last time you stepped out of your comfort zone? What was the result? How did it make you feel?

CHAPTER 5

BECOMING MORE MOTIVATED

"Successful people have the habit of doing things failures don't like to do. They don't like doing them either, but disliking is subordinated to the strength of purpose."

ALBERT GRAY, AUTHOR OF
THE COMMON DENOMINATOR OF SUCCESS

MOTIVATED SALESPEOPLE ARE HUNGRY TO MAKE THE SALE; they don't have to drag themselves out of bed in the morning. They are becoming rare these days. A 2011 study by Modern Survey discovered that 70 percent of employees are either not engaged or are under-engaged in their jobs, a record high number since the human capital measurement company began tracking these numbers in 2007. Additionally, the number of fully engaged employees has dropped to a record low of just 8 percent. This indicates a profound deterioration in the number of employees who are fully committed to their work and their organization.

This data is staggering but no surprise to business owners and sales managers operating in today's me-first culture. Managing human resources to get quality work time and effort is an issue. Temptations abound: telecommuting employees can always find better things to do such as laundry and running errands, while those in office cubicles tend to take long coffee breaks, use work time for personal e-mails, and surf the Web. Factor in that today's employees often feel entitled, not grateful, for the opportunity to work. The result: The same people who would never consider stealing anything from a department store are stealing time from their employer.

When we work with sales managers, they tell us that all they really want is an individual committed to the job; someone as committed to performance as they are. They want people like them! Their mistake is in spending most of their time with their top performers (people much like themselves). Since top performers only make up 20 percent of the team, that means managers often are ignoring 80 percent of the resources they are managing. The manager's job is to get the most out of *every* member of the team, to help people understand their personal barriers, and to create a development plan that helps each team member become a better performer. Then the manager has a full team to work with—not just one-fifth of a team.

COMMITTED EMPLOYEES ARE GOLDEN

We love to share stories of committed salespeople, and this one has a personal slant. Scott got his selling genes from his father, a straight commission organ and piano salesperson who was committed to his family of seven and to his company. Andy Anderson did not wait for his phone to ring or for customers to wander into the showroom. He was committed to making his own leads.

Many times during slow periods, when others were sitting around shooting the bull, he was writing letters, making phone calls, and basically doing anything he could to create opportunity. He was even known to go outside the Schmitt Music Store in downtown Minneapolis, stand on the street, and peer into the showroom window. When some unsuspecting passerby stopped and asked what he was doing, Andy would strike up a conversation in hopes of getting the potential customer to come in the store for an organ demonstration. This took courage as well as commitment to action.

Scott remembers his father listening to sales presentations on an old cassette player. He would stop the tape, rewind, and listen to the tape over and over until he had memorized each feature and benefit of the new product verbatim.

Not only did this commitment to preparation stick with Scott, it impressed him that his dad was doing this product homework on his personal time. You'll hear us say repeatedly throughout this book that many people want to become top performers, but few are willing to pay the price it takes to get there. Andy taught Scott at a young age what that really means.

Barriers to Motivation

Many salespeople who are unable to motivate themselves need to start by reflecting on what might be getting in the way of their motivation.

We consistently find these barriers to motivation:

◆ **Lack of purpose:** If you don't have a sense of purpose behind what you are doing, it is difficult to stay motivated.

◆ **Lack of desire:** This could be someone who has become complacent, is happy with the way things are, and has no desire to take his performance to the next level. It could also be someone who was never interested in being in sales.

◆ **Weak or no goals:** We are amazed at the number of salespeople who work in the most transparent job in the company but refuse to set goals for themselves (beyond the sales goals the company sets).

◆ **Fear of failure:** While some fear is healthy, allowing yourself to become overcome with the fear of failure can be an excuse for not pushing yourself. Author and motivational speaker Jim Rohn once said that "failure is nothing more than a few errors in judgment repeated every day."

NO REGRETS

In the movie *Dodgeball*, cyclist Lance Armstrong makes a cameo appearance to try to motivate a dejected dodgeball player (Vince Vaughn). He delivers a great line: "I guess if a person never quit when the going got tough, they wouldn't have anything to regret the rest of their lives."

Sometimes the Fire Is Lost

There are many reasons why people may lack motivation: poor management (a frequent culprit), lack of rewards (inadequate compensation structure), weak support system (associating with toxic people), lack of purpose or desire, imbalance between home and work, and fear of failure.

The Thrill of the Hunt

Some employees are more focused on getting the job than keeping it. Take Sam; he really wanted a job with Company A. In fact, he was so passionate about working for the company that he researched the routine of the hiring executive and offered to meet the executive several times at Starbucks at 5:30 a.m. when the executive stopped by for his morning jolt of java. This was a sacrifice for Sam, who lived an hour's drive away.

Initially, the executive did not feel that Sam was a great fit for the organization, but he warmed to the idea because of Sam's commitment and perseverance. If Sam brought that to the job, he would be an asset to the company. So the executive hired Sam.

As soon as Sam joined the company, it seemed as though the fire was gone. He fell back into cruise mode, his comfort zone. When the executive chanced to see Sam on business trips, he often found him working out in the hotel fitness room in the afternoon instead of making sales calls. In sales, you have to hustle, and this made the executive wonder: Where was the guy who would get up early and want to meet for coffee? How truly committed was Sam?

Despite mentoring and training, Sam never lived up to the potential he showed in the job interview. Eventually, he was phased out of the organization.

See how important motivation is? Managers would rather have someone who is committed and motivated than someone who is highly skilled but lacks motivation. At least with motivation, they have something to work with.

Remember, there is definitely pain and sacrifice in every commitment you make. There is a price you have to pay. The average person looks at the top-performing athlete or salesperson and thinks how lucky they are to be in that position. What they don't see is the commitment to excellence and the price these individuals have paid.

Burned Out

It is especially painful for a company to see a top performer fade because he has lost his motivation. Once we were called to coach a *successful* senior sales executive for a major financial organization. John (not his real name) typically made a half million dollars a year in compensation, yet lately he had been struggling and had even been put on a performance plan by his manager.

John's behaviors and skills sets were top-notch. Something wasn't adding up. The biggest red flag for us was that John was doing all the activities required to be successful in the business, but the expected results weren't there. We suspected John had simply lost his fire for the job. In the end, we learned that John felt he had been away from home too much over the years; that all he wanted to do was go back to Dallas, spend time with his family, fish, and find a local job with no travel.

Could this situation have been avoided? Yes. If John had just proactively taken a step back a year earlier and implemented strategies to reenergize his commitment, he would still be producing for his company, which would have benefited both John and his company in the long term.

As sales performance consultants, we see this all the time. It typically occurs when individuals hit their late thirties or early forties. They continue to run hard; but, when they don't see the light at the end of the tunnel or passion wanes, they lose their enthusiasm for the tasks at hand. They sometimes find the tasks that use to come easy—from filling out a report to prospecting and cold calling—hard to do.

We know the selling profession is difficult. Salespeople are on a never-ending treadmill of goals, always starting over from quarter to quarter and year to year. Most salespeople hate to hear their manager utter the demoralizing words: "We did a great job hitting the numbers this year, but don't rest on your laurels because next year we are really going to have to stretch to make quota." Some managers forget that people need time to reflect and feel good about what they accomplished before they get hit with the next challenge.

Characteristics of Motivation

Motivation is one of the four attributes we see in top performers. If an employee lacks commitment and motivation, you might as well not even spend the energy or money training him. As a company, you will see no return on investment. What qualities does a motivated salesperson have?

- **Discipline:** Motivated salespeople readily make sacrifices to meet goals, are well prepared to handle or avoid roadblocks, and do their homework so they understand their products/services, their customers, and their customers' needs.

- **Determination:** Motivated salespeople are persistent and don't take "no" for an answer. Sixty percent of customers say no four times before saying yes; 92 percent of salespeople give up after the fourth no.

- **Drive:** Motivated salespeople are driven to attain their goals, are hungry to make the sale, and create long-term goals and know how to achieve them.

- **Courage:** Motivated salespeople step out of their comfort zone and challenge themselves and others. They bend the rules to get the job done and take calculated risks to get the sale.

- **Investment:** Motivated salespeople put in the extra time and effort to complete the job, seek to continually improve themselves through training and education, are willing to "pay their dues," and make contacts to lay the foundation for future opportunities.

◆ **Purpose:** Motivated salespeople understand their personal goals, develop strategies and steps to attain them, and provide a clear understanding of why they are working.

Take a moment to look at this list. Top performers do not shy away from self-assessment. To improve, they have to be aware of their strengths and weaknesses. When it comes to motivation, we find that people often have blind spots. Which of these characteristics apply to you? Which do you wish you were stronger in?

"The difference between history's boldest accomplishments and its most staggering failures is often simply the diligent will to persevere."

ABRAHAM LINCOLN, US PRESIDENT

Let's look more closely at some of the traits that demonstrate motivation.

Discipline

When we think of discipline, we think of Bob Erkel, a guy who started selling life insurance full time in his early twenties while still taking a full course load in college. He was married with young children, which is motivation on its own. His market was not the best selling environment; the college was located in a small farming community so his prospects were tight-fisted farmers and poor students. But Bob had one thing going for him: discipline.

Northwestern Mutual Life, the company he worked for, had a disciplined sales process, which included going into the office on Monday nights to make prospect calls. As you can imagine, the hit ratio for appointments was relatively low. Still, Bob persevered, making calls in his office using, verbatim, the script the company had given the newbies (even though Bob wasn't a newbie).

Where is Bob today? He's still a top performer for Northwestern Mutual more than twenty-five years later. He was smart and disciplined enough to follow the best practices that his company laid out for him. He now has one of the largest insurance agencies in the Twin Cities, only works days (unlike many in this field working nights and weekends), has a big support staff who makes all his appointments, and targets primarily businesses and business owners. Northwestern Mutual frequently asks Bob to speak to agents across the country on how to build a successful practice.

Bob's not a flashy sales guy. For all we know, he still uses the same Samsonite briefcase and wears the same blue suit, white shirt, and red tie from college. None of that matters. What matters is that he is disciplined in his approach and focused on the execution of a strategy that his company said would work.

Insurance is a straight commission business with more than a 90 percent fallout ratio in four years. Only 10 percent of the people in this industry succeed, and Bob is one of them.

Bob exhibits, to this day, the motivation and discipline to be a top performer.

It is important to note that for every Bob Erkel there are thousands of insurance salespeople who never make it. Unlike Bob, they did not commit themselves to the activity their company prescribed. They didn't make the number of calls required, write the prospecting letters, and conduct the customer interviews that were all part of the formula for success. This is a classic example of how succeeding in sales isn't rocket science; it is merely the discipline to get it done!

Determination and Drive

The determination and drive in top-performing sales-people is evidenced by their unwillingness to give up. It isn't over until they say it's over! They love to compete and refuse to lose. This characteristic is readily found in top-performing athletes. When the game is close and the clock is running out, these athletes want the ball in their hands; they want to take the last shot or the last swing. In the case of players like Michael Jordan, Reggie Jackson, and Tom Brady, they were said to be able to will their teams to victories.

When you lose a sale how do you react? Do you say, "We'll get the next one"? Or do you say, "What will it take to still make this happen?" A client we work with received a verbal commitment for a multimillion-dollar deal with the Department of Defense (DOD). It is the type of deal that is so big that everyone in the company celebrates. Our client's competitor, however, wouldn't give up. In fact, the competitor, in an act of determination, got the decision reversed and in writing. No one would blame our client for giving up at this time, but the company didn't. Driven to want to win, our client elevated the decision to an even higher level. After many long days of effort, our client was awarded (for good this time) the business.

Courage

In selling, just as in life, courage plays an important role. We are not accountants sitting in a cubicle crunching numbers. In sales, we put our ego on the line every day and face rejection. It takes courage to call people who may not want to talk to you. It takes courage to go around individuals who want to block your progress in accounts. It takes courage to elevate your contact level and meet with senior management.

In the movie *Ferris Bueller's Day Off*, teenage Ferris was always taking risks and experiencing the full enjoyment of life. His friend Cameron, on the other hand, was always apprehensive and could only admire Ferris's ability to challenge the rules. By the end of the movie, however, awareness hits Cameron and he finds the courage to challenge his comfort zone and face his fear. It was liberating for Cameron, and regardless of the consequences, he felt alive.

Why play it safe when we know that it will take courage many times to win the deal? If we do not exhibit courage, we are left with regrets. Set challenging goals. Take calculated risks. Get the sale.

BEING BRAVE AND DOING IT YOUR WAY

Anyone who sells in a complex, buyer-controlled sales environment will appreciate this act of courage. Steve was working on a large deal selling 401k recordkeeping services to a large retailer. The decision was being managed by a third-party consultant who was calling all the shots. The consulting firm created the RFP (request for proposal) and whittled the playing field down to three companies, Steve's firm being one of them. Steve's firm had been up against this consultant many times and had never been awarded the business. Given this, Steve decided to do something courageous. He contacted the retailer directly and scheduled some insight meetings. This was not an easy decision as it went against the consultant's demand that every request for information go through the consulting company.

Steve also deviated from the consultant's agenda during his finalist presentation, deciding to present what he believed the client would want to see. He said the consultant was so ticked off during the presentation that she wouldn't even look at him. He figured he was dead in the water but felt good about the presentation, thinking that if he were going to lose another deal with this consultant, he was going to do it on his terms. Well, two weeks later he got a call from the consultant, who said, "Against my better judgment, the client is awarding you the business."

It takes courage to go around our detractors, cold call, or reach out to a high-level executive. The importance of being courageous in sales should not be underestimated.

Investment

What investments do you make in your personal and professional development? A salesperson who invests both time and money in his career is likely a top performer. He is the guy who is at work early or stays late regardless of who is watching. She is the woman who shows her commitment to success by making personal investments in her development—from taking courses to reading books.

What investments do you make in your personal and professional development?

Most senior sales executives are in their positions because they have been successful in the field. It is rare to see these individuals watching a clock; they work to get the results they want, regardless of time. Similarly, that is what they want their people doing. They want them committed, and the one thing they can observe is the amount of time they are working.

Pretending to work harder than you are doesn't gain you, or the company, anything. It is simply cheating and easy to see through. Forget your plan to strategically send e-mails at 4:00 a.m. or 11:00 p.m. to demonstrate your work ethic. Don't always be talking about how busy you are. Remember the words of Margaret Thatcher, former prime minister of the United Kingdom, "If you have to tell people you are a lady, you're not." If you have to tell people how hard you are working, you probably aren't. As the Nike commercial says, "Just do it." People will notice, and you will not only get the credit you deserve for working hard but the results as well. There always is an investment of time that is critical to success.

 TIP *Don't fly by the seat of your pants; it may take you to the wrong airport. Be focused, be disciplined, and execute your strategy to the best of your unique ability.*

Purpose

In an earlier chapter, we discussed how top performers have a purpose that helps to drive their career and motivate them. Purpose is your rudder in the water to guide you through your career.

We cannot tell you the number of business plans that cross our desk. The creators of these plans are in love with an idea, and they can't wait to make their fortune. The number who actually turn their plan into a business is small. The dream often stalls when they realize that there are no more safety nets. It is not, and will not ever be, easy to start a business. The great majority of people with entrepreneurial dreams are better off contributing 100 percent of their effort to their respective companies.

You can find your own purpose in working for someone else. That purpose could be self-actualizing if you love what you do or just the knowledge that you are providing for your family (the end result). The notion that work needs to be fun is not always a reality.

Try to find purpose in what you do but understand that it is not required that you own the business in order to be fulfilled. Try to take what you like to do and see if you can replicate it in your job, thus building a more fulfilling life and career.

We have seen many talented people fail because they won't do what the motivated person will do to be successful.

Determination and drive fuel success because they won't let you give up on your quest to be the best that you can be. Individuals who have these traits believe they own the greatest job ever—no matter what it is. A perfect example of this is Tom, a receptionist at a large company in Chicago. No matter how long it has been since we've worked with this client—even a hiatus of five years—Tom remembers us when we walk in the door: "It is great to see you again, Mr. Anderson."

Unbelievable. Stepping through the doors of that company is like seeing a long, lost friend.

To some, Tom is only the receptionist. But to most who know him, Tom is the best there is. He is truly amazing and a huge asset to the company. In fact, Tom is highly sought after by other companies; yet, he remains committed to his company and his company to him. His company even designed a customer service training program about his commitment to customer service called "The Tommy Training."

Once we asked Tom where he gets his motivation. He told us he finds people interesting, and he can always learn something from everyone he comes in contact with. He loves coming to work because of the wide range of people he gets to interface with.

Tom doesn't have to take this approach, but, by taking it, it makes his job more interesting, and thus, he can do it better. He is engaged and committed.

WHAT IS YOUR PURPOSE STATEMENT?

 TIP *If you are feeling a lack of purpose, try building a purpose statement. Start by creating a list of things you enjoy doing. Next, narrow that list by circling the items you not only enjoy doing, but do well. Lastly, develop a statement that demonstrates how you will leverage your talents as part of your work.*

As an example, when Chip is away from work, he puts on the tool belt and builds things. Building cabins, decks, and cabinets are all part of his fun. While this is a huge passion of his, he isn't going to quit his job running a sales training business tomorrow to build decks. However, there are many aspects of building that he is able to weave into his work. In fact, the same satisfaction he gets from sitting in a lawn chair after a hard day's work and looking at his finished project applies to the work he does building tools and methodology for his clients. He also thinks he is a funny guy, so not surprising his purpose statement reads: "I will leverage my sense of humor and . . ."

Maybe an example closer to home is a strategic account manager whom we recently trained. She viewed her talents as relationship building and pleasing others. Her purpose statement read: "I will leverage my sense of humor and enjoyment in pleasing others to build stronger relationships that result in better solutions to my clients' problems."

Find ways to weave the things you enjoy doing into your work. Start with the building a purpose statement exercise above.

What Motivates You?

It is difficult to coach a person who does not have the desire to get better. When we start to work with someone, we initially bucket their desire into three categories:

- ◆ **The Peak Performers:** These individuals have the desire to be the best. Their work is their favorite hobby, and they have a hard time distinguishing between work and play. These salespeople are going to succeed regardless of our training, coaching, or their situations.

◆ **The Contributors:** These individuals want to be seen as valuable to their team or organization. They do not require to be the best. They simply want to be viewed as a contributor to the team. They do their job and are consistent at achieving their quota.

◆ **The Maintainers:** These individuals are happy maintaining the status quo, comfort level, or routine. They typically stay in their comfort zone. These are the people who quit their jobs years ago but forgot to tell anyone. They do not want anyone or anything disrupting their routine.

This model can easily map to Maslow's Hierarchy of Human Needs but obviously simplified. Maslow's Hierarchy shows how humans prioritize their needs:

◆ **Physiological needs:** "The have to haves" such as food, water, temperature regulation.

◆ **Safety needs:** "The need to haves" such as maintaining a sociable, predictable, orderly, and non-threatening environment.

◆ **Love and belongingness needs:** "A want to have" that refers to the need to love and receive love in return, to be part of a group.

◆ **Self-esteem needs**: "Another want to have" that is especially necessary for top-performing salespeople.

◆ **Self-actualization needs:** "A love to have" that focuses on self-fulfillment, becoming all you are capable of becoming.

These needs motivate all human beings. The needs that are important to us will determine how much we will get out of training and how far we will go in life and in our careers.

The Peak Performer and Contributor, for example, are usually open to new ideas and coaching, if they view it as edgy or valuable and will help them do a better job of differentiating their approach. They are easier to train and get the most out of the company's investment.

The Maintainer will provide lip service and may even push back a little when presented with change (new ideas and training) but will never take action. These are the hardest people to get to take any positive action and will likely never fulfill their self-actualization needs. They are all about getting that paycheck and satisfying the physiological and safety needs of their family.

Everyone is motivated differently. Believe it or not, many of us are unaware of what our motivational drivers are. Is it a sense of purpose (see figure 6), a powerful driving force, a strong set of goals, or a sound accountability strategy?

◆ **Punitive:** Some are motivated by the "punitive" or "the stick"; they fear failure, being reprimanded (especially in front of peers), disappointing others, and being fired or demoted. While this is a negative driving force, to reach top performance there needs to be some fear of failure or perceived ramifications of failing.

- **Prize:** Some people are motivated by the carrot in front of them or "the prize": compensation, material objects, financial security and independence, and recognition and accolades that come with attaining their goals.

- **Purpose:** People who are motivated by "purpose" have a positive feeling associated with achieving their goals. Purposeful driving forces include a sense of achievement, enjoyment in pleasing others, a desire to contribute or lead, and the

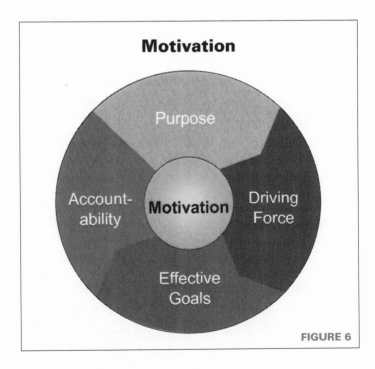

FIGURE 6

satisfaction of taking responsibility for your family or your company.

The reason it is so important to understand your own personal driving force is that it enables you to tie an effective reward to the achievement of goals. We are big believers in rewarding yourself when you hit your goals. As an example, here is how to leverage both the punitive driving force and the prize driving force: Set your goals for one year with a reward/punishment. If you do not hit your goals, you will not be allowed to play golf, which is a sport that you love. If you do succeed in your goals, you get to buy a new custom-tailored suit.

Most people are not rewarding themselves when they hit their goals. This becomes even harder as you become more successful and your driving force may change over time. When you are younger in your career and have more financial needs, the prize may take precedent as your driving force. But what about when you are financially secure? The prize may not drive your behaviors as much as purpose does. You may need to leverage other driving forces.

TRY THESE STRATEGIES TO INCREASE YOUR MOTIVATION

If your motivation is lacking, it may be because you have an ineffective driving force. Consider these strategies for creating a stronger driving force in different situations:

The "Punitive" Driving Force: While too much of a punitive driving force can be unhealthy, too little can lead to complacency. From time to time, you may need to remind yourself that you are replaceable, that you are fortunate to have a job, and that you need to work hard to keep it.

The "Prize" Driving Force: Not that life revolves around material objects, but if your motivation is broken, you may want to ask yourself if you have lost sight of the prize. As an example, each year Chip looks at the prospect of spending fifty to sixty nights away from his family each year and gets a bit down. He questions why he chose this profession. Then he quickly reminds himself of what the income from these travels means to his family. He also makes sure to reward both him and his family with a "prize." For his family, that prize may be a wintertime getaway to a tropical location; for him, the prize might be a new toy for the lake cottage or a new watch. He also recognizes that the income he generates is going toward putting his children through college, which isn't the prize but is more important and leads to the third driving force—purpose.

The "Purpose" Driving Force: If you lose sight of why you do what you do, try sitting down and making a list of everything you are thankful for. You may be surprised at how long your list becomes. You may start with your spouse, children, siblings, parents, and friends. But if you think a little harder, you'll come up with things like your business relationships, your hobbies, your talents, and your interests as examples. Try posting that list on the wall in your office. The next time you are down and questioning why you do what you do, take a look at that list—it will be a good reminder.

Motivation Strategy: Be a Goalie!

The hardest thing for an individual to do is to step back, set a strategy, and then execute it. Too many times, it is more convenient to fly by the seat of your pants and drive high levels of activity without accomplishing a thing. Or worse yet is letting your time and energy be consumed by low levels of activity such as responding to unimportant e-mails or doing busy work (filling out expense forms) instead of focusing on the tasks that get results. Top performers always find a way to do more; they set goals; they execute.

If you are struggling with motivation, goal setting weekly/monthly activities is the right strategy to start building momentum.

In the sales training business, we set goals around networking meetings (how many new people we meet with) along with new business presentations (new opportunities with prospects, typically at an executive level). These types of goals are activity goals. They are specific. If you are having trouble getting going, start by setting activity goals versus outcome goals, which are broad and general such as "I will achieve my sales quota."

 TIP *The next time you are setting goals think of these tips:*

- ◆ *Set incremental goals.*

- ◆ *Rewrite your goals frequently.*

- ◆ *Reward yourself when you meet or exceed your goals. Celebrate small successes.*

- *Manage your energy as effectively as your time.*

- *Work hard, but give yourself sufficient recovery time.*

- *Goals should stretch and help you grow. They should not be easily attainable. You should not be accomplishing 100 percent of your goals. If you are, your goals are set too low.*

- *Your goals should lead you in the right direction. This gives you a little momentum, and sometimes getting back to the basics is a great place to start.*

Conclusion

Salespeople come up with a lot of excuses why they did not hit their numbers. We understand that technology is always changing and that the internal administrative challenges never go away. However, we do not accept a missed opportunity because you procrastinated about placing a phone call or in scheduling a meeting with a prospect. This often is the result of lack of motivation.

REFLECTION EXERCISES

What are your barriers to becoming more motivated?

Do friends and colleagues refer to you as a driven and motivated person? If not, what aren't they seeing in you that would change that opinion?

What is the makeup of your driving force (i.e., punitive vs. prize vs. purpose)?

CHAPTER 6

PRACTICING PERSONAL ACCOUNTABILITY

"It is not only what we do, but also what we don't do, for which we are accountable."

MOLIÈRE, PLAYWRIGHT

VOLTAIRE ONCE SAID, "NO SNOWFLAKE IN AN AVALANCHE ever feels responsible." So much of practicing personal accountability is possessing the self-awareness to recognize the impact and influence we have on the world in which we live—and more specific to salespeople, recognizing that we are ultimately accountable for results.

People with high levels of accountability take ownership of their work and the results that are expected. In his book *Peak Performance*, Charles Garfield explained that in all his research, he found that people are not born top performers; they are made into them. In other words, the belief that someone is just born to be superior is a fallacy.

He also found that top performers are not superhuman people with incredible talents; they are average people like you and us. And finally, he states that they are not workaholics but people who are committed to results.

Sales managers want their reps to have accountability. They know the ones with high accountability will figure out a way to reach their goals and quota. Top reps understand what they control and what to focus on. They understand that success comes from the "right" activity, the "right" size of deal, and the "right" close ratio. If any one of these criteria is not met, top reps understand they must increase the ratio. For example, if you did not meet your sales quota, you have to ask yourself, did you do enough of the right activity? If yes, did you pursue the right size opportunities? If yes, then you didn't close enough deals. Top performers take ownership of their sales goals and their results—both good and bad.

Accountability is one of the reason's top salespeople are the easiest to train. They want to get better and understand it is their responsibility to the organization to continue to improve.

Barriers to Accountability

Salespeople who lack a sense of accountability, on the other hand, are difficult to train because they do not accept responsibility for their actions. If nothing is their fault or responsibility, then what motivation do they have to improve? The following barriers keep salespeople from developing a sense of accountability:

◆ **Awareness:** Some people do not realize that they are not being accountable. They are unaware a problem even exists. Remember, the same set of skills that is required for competency is the same set of skills required to *recognize competency.* Those with low self-awareness may need help from a loved one or a manager to point out the fact that accountability is an area that needs development.

◆ **Unwillingness to take ownership:** "It's not my job" or "Someone else should have to take a turn doing this" are examples of an unwillingness to take ownership. In his early years as a politician, former President George H.W. Bush (the first President Bush) lost his bid for a seat in Congress representing Texas. On election night, he turned to his supporters during his concession speech and said, "It's my fault." Years later, when he lost the White House to Bill Clinton, he did the same thing. He told supporters and staff, "It's my fault." Was it entirely Bush's fault that he didn't win reelection? Of course not. However, his willingness to take ownership of the defeat speaks greatly to the character of the man and showed he had a sense of accountability.

◆ **No ramifications:** What if there were never any ramifications to our actions? What if no one was ever held accountable for what they did? The prisons are full of people who believed they could get away with something without ramification. The classic example is the family on the summer vacation. The kids are in the back of the minivan fighting and making too much noise. Dad yells back to them, "If you kids don't knock it off, I am going to pull this car over." In all the years of saying this to kids, how often do parents pull the car over? You guessed it, rarely. The point is that there were no real ramifications to the kids' misbehavior, and they knew it. Without ramification, there is chaos—whether in a society or in a family. If you believe there are no ramifications to your actions, then you will never be a top performer.

♦ **Lack of support system:** If we fail to utilize our friends, coworkers, and colleagues to hold us accountable, we are missing out. Too many people do not share their goals and aspirations with others for fear of being embarrassed when they don't accomplish them. They forget that, for the most part, people are supportive. They want to help you reach your goals if they can.

ACCOUNTABLE PEOPLE NEVER QUIT

Chip's father-in-law, Chuck LaGow, is a testament to this. Growing up in a rural area, he did not have the benefit of higher education. He was fortunate to get a job sweeping floors at a lumberyard. Through years of hard work, he ended up running this business and buying out the owner. Along the way, he also built a successful real estate development company and a property management company. On the surface, he does not appear to possess any special talents or superhuman powers. What Chip has observed about his father-in-law over the years, though, is an incredible will to win. His personal accountability for results drove him to succeed in many different business ventures.

Top Performers Hold Themselves Accountable

Accountability is all about ownership. It is one of the attributes of top performers. People with high levels of accountability have these traits:

- **Accept total responsibility for results.** Top performers do not play the blame game. They accept responsibility for results when things go wrong, when they don't land that important account, when they give a disappointing presentation, or when their numbers slide. By stepping up and taking responsibility, they gain power—the power to cause change and to turn the results around.

- **Do not rely on excuses.** Those with high levels of accountability do not make excuses. In fact, they tend to swing too far on the opposite end of the pendulum, often being *too* hard on themselves and *too* quick to blame themselves.

- **Are responsible for their own happiness.** Accountable people do not feel that it is other people's responsibility to make them happy. They believe they have a right to be happy and work proactively to create a lifestyle that allows it. In the movie *Pursuit of Happyness,* which is based on a true story, Chris Gardner (played by Will Smith) falls on hard times. A single parent with a five-year-old son, he loses his job and has no safety net to fall back on. He and his son are on the streets, fighting for a spot in line at a homeless shelter and spending the night in fear behind the locked doors of a metro station bathroom. In one of his monologues, Gardner points out that our founding fathers never guaranteed happiness. All they guaranteed to each of us is "the pursuit of happiness" and that it is up to each of us to be responsible for finding happiness. And you know what? Chris Gardner went from a struggling salesperson to a Wall Street legend.

- ◆ **Accept total responsibility for results.** They accept total responsibility for results and are not looking for someone to blame. At the time of the writing of this book, there was a protest movement called "Occupy Wall Street." These protesters were upset with what they believed is an unfair distribution of wealth in our country. While the movement has gotten traction in different parts of the country, there remains to be much confusion over what the protesters are actually asking for. In fact, one of their protest chants was: "We don't know what we want, but we want it now!" Interviews with protesters revealed a number of heart-breaking stories of hard-working people being laid off from their jobs and not being able to provide for their families. The question, though, is how constructive is it to camp out in a city park each day and night in protest? They want to hold Wall Street, or the government, or our capitalist system responsible for their current situation. How will this help them get back on their feet? Wouldn't they benefit more by taking this same sense of conviction and applying it to getting re-employed—perhaps camping out on the doorstep of the company they would like to get a job with to show their commitment?

◆ **Are disciplined in their approach.** Discipline helps top performers focus on results. We talked about discipline in chapter 5 and how it is a key characteristic of someone who is highly motivated. It is also a characteristic of the accountable salesperson. When you hold yourself accountable, you are committed to getting things done, and that takes discipline.

◆ **Believe they have control of the result.** When we look at accountability, we are really looking at varying levels of control or responsibility. "Full control" represents things you have complete control over, "indirect control" are things that you have some control over, and "no control" represents outcomes that you have no influence or control over. Top performers focus their energy on those items they have full or indirect control over proportionally. They don't waste time worrying about the things they can't control.

As a salesperson or account manager think about the many factors you have control over:

- Providing the best possible customer service and customer experience

- Timely communication, even when it isn't good news

- Positioning the value of your solution (before you position price)

- Going beyond the traditional needs analysis and really understanding the customer's business

- Networking for new opportunities

- Knowing your own products and services inside and out

- Understanding how to move the customer through the selling process

In the sales environment many of us operate in, you can sometimes feel out of control of the customer's buying process as they put together and hire consultants to interact with their vendors. Instead of fretting about things you can't affect, think about this long list of actions and results you can control.

Strategies for Raising Your Level of Accountability

Here are some strategies to help you raise your level of accountability:

♦ **Journal:** Nutritionists say those who write down what they eat are twice as likely to stick to their diet. The same can be said for exercise. Keeping track of your workouts each week in a journal will inspire you to get to the gym more often. Journaling is also a great strategy for improving your time management. Try this for a week. At the end of each day take five to ten minutes to write down everything you did that day. Be as specific as possible, breaking your day into small increments. On the first day, this data will have little meaning, but over the course of several days of journaling, you will begin to see patterns in your behavior that may need to be corrected.

♦ **Create accountability teams:** Several years ago, we started dividing participants in our training workshops into accountability teams. Your accountability teammates are responsible for holding you accountable for the goals you set for yourself. This has proven to be a powerful tool for getting people to take what they've learned in the training workshops and apply them in the field. We ask training workshop participants to keep these accountability teams intact for ninety days, but find that many of them continue to correspond with their teams long after, which no doubt is a testament to the value of the teams and their ability to help in holding people accountable. Weight Watchers uses a similar strategy. It has found that those who attend the meetings regularly lose 50 percent more weight than other members. Support and peer pressure are incredibly powerful accountability mechanisms.

- **Practice personal accountability:** There is a great definition for the word "authentic" that fits well here: *authentic—who you are when no one is watching.* We make a thousand decisions a day in work and in our personal life. When you do the right thing, even when no one can see you, you are being accountable.

- **Focus on what you can control:** As we already discussed, spending time worrying about things you cannot control or influence is a waste of time and energy—time and energy that could be applied to the things you can control and influence.

- **Set effective goals:** It never ceases to amaze us at how ineffective many professionals are at setting goals for themselves. Make sure all of your goals are S.M.A.R.T. goals. We are advocates of the S.M.A.R.T. goal principles with one minor change—the "A" for "Attainable" should be changed to "A Stretch." The entire acronym looks like this:

  - ❖ **S—Specific:** Make sure your goals are tangible and specific. In a goal that is too vague or general such as "I want to become a better communicator," it will be difficult to measure your progress. A better goal might be: "I am going to find more opportunities to speak or present."

❖ **M—Measurable:** A goal has to be measurable to be legitimate. Taking the previous example one step further, add an element of measurement to your goal: "I am going to find one opportunity to present or speak each month."

❖ **A—A Stretch:** Push yourself to bigger and better goals.

❖ **R—Realistic:** It is important to always do a reality check and make sure you aren't setting yourself up for failure. There is a fine line between a stretch goal and an unrealistic goal. This is where a mentor can really help out. For example, Allie had her heart set on becoming a consultant after she finished her undergraduate degree. Her mentor had to delicately explain that it is unrealistic to become a consultant until you have had practical experience in a particular field. This was a tough pill for Allie to swallow, but it helped steer her toward more realistic goals and actual employment opportunities. And someday, Allie may reach her pie-in-the-sky goal of being a consultant, but first she will need to meet several other goals.

❖ **T—Timebound:** Part of a measurable goal is one with a clear start date and completion date.

> In other words, "I will find one opportunity to speak or present per month over the next six months."

Business studies have found that top performers only achieve 50 percent of their goals. What is this telling us? That top performers set lofty goals for themselves. Artist and sculptor Michelangelo once said, "The greater danger for most of us lies not in setting our aim too high and falling short, but in setting our aim too low and achieving our mark."

LEVERAGING PERSONAL ACCOUNTABILITY TO BE SUCCESSFUL

Colin Sievers owns one of the most successful automobile dealerships in the Twin Cities. Colin takes personal responsibility for everything that happens at the dealership, which is partly why he has such a loyal and, some would say, fanatic following. He built his business from the ground up starting with a small lot and one employee and growing it into a large award-winning operation. The secret to his success from his perspective is outworking the competitors to find the best cars and providing each customer with an exceptional customer experience.

Colin has little patience for employees who do not overdeliver to the company's most critical asset—the customer. He holds himself and each employee accountable to these same values.

Conclusion

Accountability is about stepping up and doing what is right. It is an attribute that is within everyone's reach.

 TIP *As you think about accountability, consider these tips:*

♦ *Make no excuses.*

♦ *Own your results when they are both good and bad.*

♦ *Take ownership of your sales goals.*

♦ *Don't ask "why" or "who" questions; ask "how" and "what" questions—as in "How can I help?" or "What can I do?"*

♦ *Keep a daily journal to create awareness of your behaviors.*

REFLECTION EXERCISES

How do I react when things go wrong? Is my first thought to blame someone else? Why?

Do I take responsibility for my successes and failures?

What can I do to increase my levels of accountability?

What have I done to improve my performance?

CHAPTER 7

THE IMPACT OF HIGH INTEGRITY

"Integrity is something you are given for free, but once lost, it is expensive to retrieve."

ANONYMOUS

YOU HAVE NOTHING WITHOUT INTEGRITY. Integrity leads to trust, and trust is essential for a salesperson. People buy from people they trust.

Integrity is built on consistency and perception. So why do some salespeople persist in shooting themselves in the foot by taking actions that detract from trust? Simple behaviors can undermine your integrity—behaviors such as not showing up to meetings prepared or on time, not returning calls in a timely manner, or not keeping commitments.

Show Me the Trust!

It's simple. Integrity builds sales.

Today the salesperson is part of the product, especially in the case of large sales. You need to make it safe for the customer to do business with you by being the professional who covers all the bases.

A study by Achieve Global breaks down the factors most critical to customers—these are the things that build customer commitment:

◆ Business expertise and image were at the top: 29 percent

◆ Dedication to the customer: 25 percent

◆ Account sensitivity: 23 percent

◆ Product performance: 10 percent

◆ Service department excellence: 9 percent

◆ Confirmation of capabilities: 4 percent

In short, the salesperson or the account manager controls 77 percent of why companies do business with them! That's right. The human element is often what makes or breaks a sale. And who is in charge of the human element? You.

Oddly enough, this study has been hard for many salespeople to swallow. In fact, when we present this data, it is always the top performers who say, "Right on, of course, I am the reason the customer does business with us." While the underperformer will shake his head and say, "That might be true in other industries but not so much here. Price is the big factor in my business."

Is it really? Let's look at why customers leave and why you lose business.

A study conducted by the Forum Corporation discovered that customers leave for the following reasons:

- ◆ 15 percent find a better product.

- ◆ 15 percent find a less expensive product.

- ◆ 20 percent feel a lack of contact and individual attention.

- ◆ 49 percent say contact from the supplier's personnel was of poor quality.

Interestingly enough, if you ask most salespeople why they lose a sale, they will say it is price. But the Forum Corporation study indicates price is only a factor in 15 percent of lost business, **while nearly 70 percent of customers defect because they don't like the human side of doing business with a particular company.**

That's a huge disconnect. The easiest response for a customer is to say, "The price is too high," rather than telling the salesperson the truth: "We decided to go with your competitor because they were much more prepared each time they met with us."

 TIP *Integrity is why top salespeople drive a significant amount of their business through referrals.*

Throw a Little Seasoning into the Mix

Often when a salesperson scores low in integrity, it is an indication of not one big thing but many small things getting away from him. He's missing commitments. He's not listening effectively to the customers. He hasn't taken the time to understand the customer's business.

The seasoned salesperson knows that in today's world of sales it takes an intimate understanding of the customer's business to close the sale. Reading annual reports and perusing websites used to be enough to get the ball rolling. Not any longer. Competition is keener than ever before, money is tighter, personnel are wearing more hats than ever, companies are smarter at buying goods and services, and managers are demanding results yesterday.

Value and trust are paramount to developing and sustaining customer relationships. You need to demonstrate integrity and accountability to your clients. That takes more than reading background material. You need to show them that extra mile you are prepared to go for them.

LESSONS FROM A GREAT SALESMAN

We've already talked about Andy Anderson, a superstar salesman. He worked for more than forty years at Schmitt Music Company in Minneapolis, Minnesota, selling pianos and organs. During that time, he received numerous top salesman of the year awards and was profiled in several industry articles. How did he do it?

Now in his eighties and retired, Andy will tell anyone willing to listen that his integrity is how he built his successful career. Here's an example:

When he was in the Air Force performing the menial task of cleaning up a dental office, Andy broke the dental chair. No one else was around to see it. He was the only one who would have ever known that he broke the chair while cleaning it. Even back then, dental chairs were expensive. The consequences of owning up to breaking it weren't appealing.

When the colonel came into the office for inspection the next day, he immediately noticed the broken chair. He demanded to know who had broken his (the government's) expensive chair. Without hesitation, Andy stepped forward.

"Sir, I did."

Andy demonstrated his level of integrity and trust despite the threat of immediate consequences. He is convinced that taking accountability for the broken chair ultimately jump-started his military career. The colonel was impressed. He became like a father figure to Andy, continuing to hand out more responsibility and meritorious promotions. Andy was someone he could trust. In four short years, Andy left the military at the rank of staff sergeant, which is quite an accomplishment.

That integrity value was the driver that helped Andy become one of the top-performing salespeople in the piano and organ business. It enabled him to feed a family of seven on a straight commission compensation structure. His integrity drove a continuous stream of repeat customers and referrals, ultimately leading to his ability to travel the world and live a comfortable retirement.

To this day, Andy Anderson's word is gold, as it should be for every salesperson.

Barriers to Integrity

In our training workshops, we show a list of possible barriers to integrity and ask participants to rank the barriers that resonate with them. With a sample size of many hundreds of reps, it is interesting to see which barriers rose to the top:

- **Competing priorities:** Many felt this barrier to high integrity was due to the fact that priorities set by their company often competed with the priority of building integrity with the customer. For example, a push to get sales in before the end of a quarter could convince a rep to push the customer too hard for the order.

- **Lack of time management:** Think about the times that you have been guilty of doing something that diminishes your integrity with a customer. Whether it was inadvertently typing the wrong customer name on a proposal or providing inaccurate information, there was probably a good chance you were stretched trying to do too many things at once.

- **Corporate culture:** Many sales professionals believe the lack of integrity demonstrated by their own company was a barrier to their integrity. This really reveals the importance of companies to recognize that their actions set the tone for how their employees behave.

Your Word Is Ultimately All You Have

The old adage is true. "You can't make a good deal with a bad person." You probably have met people who lack integrity. Maybe they brag about taking a personal vacation with company money, or how they constantly pull the wool over their boss's eyes. If they will cheat on their company, they will cheat on you. The best way to address your own integrity is to have people hold you accountable. If you make a commitment, keep it regardless of the inconvenience.

Remember, the customer is always asking herself, "Can I trust this salesperson and/or can I trust this company?" A salesperson's integrity is broken down into:

- **Personal integrity:** Your personal integrity consists of your morals, values, and ethics. As we discussed in the personal accountability chapter, it is who you are when no one else is around. It is your authentic self.

- **Professional integrity:** This is your approach to your job, business ethics, and credibility.

You Can Easily Damage Your Personal Integrity

You typically get one time to demonstrate your integrity to a customer. If you fail the test, you will most likely lose the customer. There are few do-overs in sales. Your personal integrity is harder to define and observe than professional integrity, which is exhibited through observable behaviors. Here are examples of behaviors that eat away at your personal integrity:

◆ **Ethical lapses:** Doing what you know is wrong. The morning paper is full of individuals justifying, by whatever means, their shortcuts to success. However, these individuals rarely have long-term relationships because of the way they conduct business.

◆ **Being phony:** When you behave one way in front of certain individuals while just the opposite in front of others, you are not being authentic. We endorse "faking it until you make it" when it comes to confidence because that can eventually lead you to become more confident—but this is never a good policy in relationship building. Faking it should never be a way of life. Faking it essentially involves lying to yourself about who you are. It is misrepresenting your résumé, your experiences, and your interest in others when you are not interested. Being a phony is a tough act to keep up and one your customers will see through in the end.

◆ **Disregard for the feelings of others:** This is deciding it is your right to say what you believe is true regardless of the feelings of others. You hide behind your "honesty" to take a shot at someone personally. You justify your actions by saying, "I am only trying to help this person out." Is that really true? Before you start gossiping behind someone's back, take a moment and wonder: if I weren't here, what would they be saying about me?

- **Not doing what you say:** Some people only live up to the commitments they make if it is convenient for them. These individuals make a commitment to meet somewhere for lunch or dinner and then only show up half the time. This is the fastest way to kill a trusting relationship in selling and account management. Make sure you write down your commitments in your calendar—both the tasks and the time frame.

- **Misrepresenting facts:** There is an old saying: "Never let the facts get in the way of a good story." As sales professionals, it is easy to fall into the trap of only giving the customer the information that lends itself to a decision in our favor. We need to recognize that there is a fine line between withholding information and misrepresenting the information.

- **Dishonesty:** This should be a no-brainer. Lying is the quickest way to lose someone's trust. The more often we lie, the more we are likely to accept this as an appropriate course of action and do it again and again.

FACT CHECKERS ARE EVERYWHERE

There was a sales manager who was excellent at pumping up his team. However, through the process, he tended to embellish the truth a bit. After one such session, one of his team members actually checked the facts that he'd been spouting and found that they did not add up. Instead of addressing it directly with the

sales manager, the team member discussed his find-
ings with the rest of the team. (The salesperson wanted
to avoid a confrontation with the manager, who was
highly emotional and known to lack composure in difficult settings—another integrity issue.) At the next team
meeting, others began checking the manager's facts.
They found more discrepancies.

Soon, the team was taking nearly anything the manager said with a grain of salt. In the end, the team saw the
manager's behavior as a matter of integrity and not just
an overzealous means of revving up the troops. The top
performers left the organization, leaving the sales manager with a mediocre team of average performers who
stayed because they had no other place to go.

Top performers show integrity and expect it from
others.

Ways to Sabotage Your Professional Integrity

How you handle yourself professionally can impact your
credibility with your customers. Study this list carefully
and with an honest heart. Are you doing any of these behaviors, which can sabotage your integrity as well as your
customer relationships?

- **Overpromising and underdelivering:** Don't
  promise the stars. Keep expectations realistic, then
  when you deliver more than you promised in less
  time than you predicted, you will win a customer
  for life. Customers remember when they are pleas-
  antly surprised by great service and dedication.

◆ **Not being prepared:** Do you show up for meet-ings without even completing the most basic homework on the customer. This tells customers that you don't even care enough to learn more about their company. Take the time to visit the company website and peruse all the available infor-mation on the customer.

◆ **Lacking a sense of urgency:** Returning phone calls or e-mails in a timely manner is a must in sales. Opportunities can be lost in a snap. Even though you are inundated with requests (aren't we all busy?), there is no excuse for a salesperson not to respond in a timely manner to a prospect or customer. Displaying a lack of urgency brings into question how much you really want the customer's business.

◆ **Consistently late for meetings:** This is calendar integrity and seems to be an epidemic in the cur-rent age. If you can't make a meeting on time, why would your customer think you can deliver a prod-uct on time? Routinely being late for meetings also says something about the value you place on your customer's time. Be respectful of the customer's time by being on time. If it is an emergency and you absolutely must be late, have the courtesy to call your customer and explain. Give your custom-er the option of waiting for you or rescheduling at the customer's convenience.

◆ **Sloppy work:** Customers notice inattention to detail. Have you ever been rushing and inserted the wrong company name and/or logo in a presentation? How do you think that makes the customer feel? Details can make or break a deal. Pay attention.

◆ **Ineffective questions:** When making a purchase, customers want you to ask them questions and be their consultant. They trust you to match them with the right product or service. You owe it to the customer to know the types of questions that will lead to making a better recommendation on a product or service.

◆ **Not listening:** This is the biggest trust buster. Poor listeners are seen as disinterested, self-absorbed, and unaware. We knew a salesperson who asked excellent questions on his first meeting but didn't listen to the answers. On the second meeting with the same customer, he asked the same questions. On the third meeting, he again asked the same questions. Finally, the customer said, "You're wasting my time; we can't do business together."

Shut Up and Listen to Build Relationships

Effective listening is a simple principle that creates a significant bond. It is crucial to building relationships and one of the most difficult skills to master.

Most salespeople consider themselves great listeners, when few really are.

Most think they create value when they talk, when most of the value is created by asking insightful questions and listening attentively to the answers.

Take the example of Alex. After a recent business meeting, his colleague took him aside and said, "Do you know how many times you interrupted our customer in that meeting? Six times! And the meeting was only forty-five minutes long."

Alex was surprised. He didn't realize that he had been talking over the customer and rudely interrupting him, repeatedly. "Sorry, but ideas pop into my head, and I just blurt them out," Alex said.

Over the next days and months, Alex became increasingly aware of how much he interrupted people, from customers to family and friends. He wanted to break this habit, but how?

Finally, Alex came up with a strategy. He wrote "shut up and listen" at the top of his legal pad prior to each meeting. This simple approach made him conscious that he needed to listen more effectively one meeting at a time.

When Mike Wallace of *60 Minutes* appeared on the *Tonight Show*, Jay Leno remarked that people who listen for a living tend to have the most interesting things to say. It's true. Once we were at a customer dinner with the senior executives of an insurance company. It was a pleasurable event, and the person who made it enjoyable was a certain executive who possessed the ability to ask great questions and then really listen to the answers. When we were able to turn the conversation toward him, we found him fascinating. His incredible sales career was studded with insights learned through listening.

Trust Is Not Negotiable; Cheaters Never Win

Golf is the one sport that you can call a penalty on yourself. It is the ultimate test of one's integrity. Consider how much business is conducted on the golf course, where your integrity or lack of integrity really shows. We cannot tell you how many times we have observed people cheating in the game of golf—from the minister who gave himself a favorable lie on every hole and never took a penalty stroke to the accountant who continually recorded scores lower than he shot. Would you feel good about attending that minister's church? Would you want that accountant balancing your books?

 TIP *If someone cheats in one area, they will cheat in others.*

Strategies for Increasing Integrity in Professional Relationships

Now that we've reviewed some key barriers to integrity as well as what can damage your integrity, let's examine some tactics that you can deploy in your selling and account management efforts that can increase integrity with customers:

- **Make sure your customers know that they are always in your thoughts:** This may seem like a little thing, but how often do customers feel like a salesperson is only focused on them when they are sitting toe-to-toe in a meeting? Start thinking about your customers and what is happening in their businesses, what you can do to improve their situation. Say things like "I was speaking to one of our solution specialists the other day about your problems with mobile computing, and he suggested you consider . . " This sends an important message that, as their salesperson (or account manager), you are thinking about their best interests, even when you are away from them.

- **Recommend solutions proactively:** Don't get caught up just reacting to their requests for product information and pricing. Try to anticipate your customers' problems.

- **Recommend solutions that aren't yours:** If you want to really increase your integrity with a customer, recommend a solution that isn't yours. We don't mean point them to a competitor, but maybe there is a solution that doesn't compete with yours that could bring value to your customer. When your customer realizes that you put in time and energy getting him a solution, even though you are not benefitting financially from it, your integrity will soar.

- **Never, never bash the competition:** There is no way around it, if you put down the competition, it will ultimately reflect badly on you. Let your competitors play that game. You take the high road. If you do a good job focusing on what differentiates you from your competition, you will put the right questions in the customer's mind and he or she can take it from there.

Conclusion

Once you lose someone's trust, it is hard to get it back. Integrity is trust. This is one of the easiest of attributes to change but the most difficult to be aware of and to acknowledge as a personal issue. Think about your actions and behaviors. Do you exhibit both personal and business integrity?

REFLECTION EXERCISES

1. What impacts your integrity?

2. What effect does becoming stressed or over-whelmed have on your strategy?

3. What do you do in your professional relationships to try to elevate the perception of your integrity?

CHAPTER 8

PRACTICAL APPLICATION: HOW DO I USE THIS BOOK AS A DEVELOPMENT TOOL?

"What gets measured, gets done."

PETER DRUCKER

THROUGHOUT THIS BOOK WE HAVE OFFERED TIPS, IDEAS, and reflection exercises to not only improve your performance as a sales or account management professional, but to also improve and find more enjoyment in all facets of life. Here are some final thoughts on how to put this book to practical use as a workbook for your professional development.

Chapters 1-3: Keys to Behavior Change, Top Performer's Tipping Point, and Are You Ready to Improve?

Review the reflection questions at the end of chapter 1. Be honest with yourself and answer the tough question of what is holding you back from taking your performance to the next level? Then, brainstorm things you can do (that are within your control) to address this barrier. If your barrier is time management, hone in on exactly what it is that is getting in the way of effective time management. Is it your ability to effectively prioritize activities? If so, set some goals for yourself around spending time each morning prioritizing your day.

In chapter 2, review the Top Performer's Tipping Point model. In this chapter, we discussed the fact that top performers aren't perfect, but they achieve a tipping point in which they have enough of the right skills and attributes to be successful. Reflect on your skills, attitude, motivation, integrity, and accountability. What are your strengths and weaknesses in each of these categories? What do you need to improve on in order to achieve your own personal tipping point?

In chapter 3, we outlined an individual's "readiness for improvement." If you have made it this far in the book, you are serious about changing your behavior, so this may not be an issue. The bigger issue may be if you have accurately self-assessed your areas of improvement. Consider using assessment tools and feedback from peers to shore up your perspective of your areas for development.

For example, clients who attend our intensive professional development workshops are required to complete two self-assessments: one on their selling skills and one on their attributes. Their manager also assesses their selling skills. In our workshops, we show participants how to use these assessment results to focus on their key areas of development. We have seen many times the surprised look on a salesperson's face when he sees a score from his manager that differs with his opinion of himself. For some, at first they become defensive and reject the feedback. But once they calm down, they go to their boss to discuss why their manager scored them so low. This discussion is an important development dialogue that needs to take place between a manager and a rep—you both put together an accurate picture of your current state (skills, attributes, performance) and what needs to happen to get to your future desired state.

Finally, set a goal for yourself to take your performance to the next level. Seek out feedback from those whom you respect and come up with two to three things to improve on (or do more of) that will make the biggest impact on your ability to take your performance to the next level. Write these as goals and post them on the wall in your office. Next determine which activity-based goals you need to achieve in support of the overall goals. For example, if your overall goal is to "step out of your comfort zone more often," your activity-based goals in support of this could be to "identify five new prospects in the next thirty days" or "get my pilot's license by the end of the year." Revisiting the four chapters on attitude, motivation, accountability, and integrity may help you come up with additional goals to add to your list.

Chapter 4: Having the Right Attitude

In this chapter, we discussed the importance of knowing what impacts your attitude both positively and negatively. Go back and review the reflection exercise questions at the end of chapter 4.

The exercise asks you to list one thing you can do to impact your attitude in three different categories: mentally, physically, and spiritually. Take this list and try to set at least one goal in each of these areas:

- **Mentally:** This consists of becoming more self-aware of what affects your attitude. Strategies discussed in this chapter included changing your circumstances if you are, for example, consuming the wrong media. It also referred to your ability to celebrate incremental successes and using positive self-talk.

- **Physically:** This section focused on the importance of recognizing that we need to take care of our bodies in order to maintain a positive attitude. This could mean giving yourself a new look, maintaining an exercise regimen, eating right, and drinking right.

- **Spiritually:** Spirituality means different things to different people. It may mean getting more involved in your church or mentoring someone in need or volunteering your time.

You may also want to set a goal for yourself regarding something you want to develop more self-confidence in.

Chapter 5: Becoming More Motivated

In this chapter, we first looked at barriers to becoming more motivated. Review these barriers. Determine your biggest barriers. What are you willing to do to address and/or find solutions to these barriers? Review the characteristics of motivated people. Which characteristics are strengths for you? Which are areas of weakness?

Review the "Three P's of Driving Force": punitive, prize, and purpose. Determine what each of these mean to you:

- **Punitive:** While you don't want to be consumed by the punitive, create consequences for underperforming and adhere to them.

- **Prize:** Determine what the "prize" is for accomplishing your goals. For example, buying a new putter when you book five new business presentations. Use the goals you set for yourself throughout this book and see if you can come up with a sufficient prize for each.

- **Purpose:** Make a list of everything you are thankful for. Post this list on your wall. Also, build a purpose statement for yourself. Make this purpose statement a reflection of what you are good at and what you enjoy doing.

Chapter 6: Practicing Personal Accountability

Chapter 6 examined how top performers are accountable and focus on those things they have control or influence over. As you reflect on this chapter, consider your own levels of accountability. Do you take ownership for your results, both good and bad? Do you take ownership of driving the right levels of activity? If accountability is an area of development for you, you may want to start by identifying the things that stand in the way of being more accountable. You may also want to review some strategies including:

- **Journaling:** Track your daily activities.

- **Creating accountability teams:** Team up with some peers to help each other be accountable.

- **Setting effective goals:** Make goals tangible, specific, and measurable.

Chapter 7: The Impact of High Integrity

Chapter 7 really focused on the important role integrity plays in building and maintaining strong professional relationships. No one wants to think that his or her integrity may be low, but often times it is the little things that eat away at our integrity. Things like getting caught in a small lie, turning in sloppy work, or not being prepared for a customer meeting. We also discussed how it is easy to have good integrity when times are good and how integrity can be challenged when times are tough. Reflect on situations you have been in that have tested your integrity, how did you do? Also, review the behaviors that damage integrity and honestly reflect on those that you may be guilty of:

- **Personal integrity:** Ethical lapses, being phony, disregard for the feelings of others, not doing what you say, misrepresenting facts.

- **Professional integrity:** Overpromising and underdelivering, not being prepared, lacking a sense of urgency, being late for meetings, sloppy work, ineffective questions, not listening.

Once you have isolated some of these behaviors, develop a plan for how to work on integrity issues as a specific goal. For instance, "I am going to spend sixty minutes of prep time for each customer meeting" (to address not being prepared).

We also discussed some strategies in this chapter that you can implement proactively to drive up the customer's perception of your integrity. Review these strategies. Identify one that you could do more of and set a goal around this as well. For instance, "I am going to proactively recommend a solution for my top five customers."

Wrap Up

We have been conducting sales training for a good portion of our adult lives. We have had the privilege to be working with the most vital and integral part of any organization—the people whose job it is to persuade others to use their company's products and services. Salespeople are the lifeline of an organization and many times are the face of the company to the world. Often, they are the reason for the company either hiring to support growth or downsizing. They are a company's most important asset and should be treated as such. They also should be invested in to ensure this asset produces at full value.

For years, we focused as an organization on skill development, assuming everyone would take the ball and run with it on their own. For those salespeople with the right attributes, the return on investment in the classroom and field was high; we got excellent business results. However, we knew there was something missing from a development perspective. We continued to ask ourselves: What is the missing link? What is the DNA of top performers and can we understand all the variables and train to them? What role does one's attributes play in success vs. skill?

We hope that, by now, you have experienced what we believe are the attributes of top performers. We recognize that our development process is unique. We understand that attributes such as attitude, motivation, integrity, and accountability are behaviors that do not change overnight. That is exactly why we showed you what these attributes look like in practice and what typical barriers keep salespeople from fully embracing these attributes. This approach wasn't intended to be negative but to take into account what happens in "real life" and not theories in a book. Reading a book can create some awareness, but it will not result in performance improvement unless you take action.

How important are the attributes to success? They are essentially the foundation of an engaged employee. Ask any manager of people if he wants someone who is highly skilled who is disengaged or someone who is less skilled but engaged? Nine out of ten managers will take the engaged employee. Why? While the engaged employee may not have skill, he will work hard to get the skills he needs. He will do the difficult things required in the job.

Such employees work hard. They contribute. They are more enjoyable to be around, and they want to earn their money.

Our work with our clients has been to provide a road map for individuals to become both highly skilled and to exhibit high levels of attributes. The bottom line in all development is a manager can't want something for you more than you want it. You need to want to get better. By improving behaviors in these key attributes, you will be on your way to a successful sales career.

CHAPTER 9

WHY SKILLS STILL MATTER

"The harder you practice, the luckier you get."

GARY PLAYER, PROFESSIONAL GOLFER

WE HAVE SPENT MUCH OF THIS BOOK EXPLAINING how attributes play a more predominant role in someone's success than skills. (In chapter 2, we reviewed a study that showed that sales executives view skills as a much lower indicator of success as compared to attributes such as attitude, motivation, accountability, and integrity.) While skills pale in comparison to the importance of our attributes in order to be successful in sales, skills *do* matter and *how* you sell does matter. In this chapter, we will help put skills in perspective and summarize those key elements of selling skills that can really make a difference.

Before we do this, reflect on all of the selling skills seminars you have ever attended, every book you have ever read on selling. Think about it, thousands of books have been written on how to sell more effectively. If you read enough of them, they all start to sound the same after awhile—you need to get to the decision maker; you need to develop a coach; you need to ask better questions. We periodically meet a sales executive who is all pumped up about a new book on selling that he views as revolutionary. We give it a quick read and see the same old concepts regurgitated with different terms and examples. How many different selling methodologies has your company been through? Miller-Heiman, Spin Selling, Counselor Selling—companies roll out these off-the-shelf training modules telling their reps that "this is the way we are going to sell" and then two years later they are moving on to something else.

Companies try to simplify and standardize the process. They reduce selling to "five steps" or "seven steps" and then train their reps on each step, only to find months later that no one remembers what step 4 was. Selling isn't about steps or tricks or funny acronyms. There is no silver bullet or "secret sauce" in all of those books on selling you see on the racks in the airport bookstores.

Selling is about executing the same universally agreed upon selling strategies better than your competition.

We Play the Perception Game

Ever notice in sales that it really comes down to perceptions? It is never how good you are; it is the customer's perception of how good you are. It is never how high your prices are; it is the customer's perception of how high your prices are. We play the perception game, and that is why our profession is so interesting and challenging at times. If you've worked with a customer long enough, he has developed a perception of you, your company, and your solutions. If you have done a good job of establishing the value you are bringing to your customer's business through your interactions, you may be seen as a solution provider or a valued resource. Your business relationship is a two-way street working in cooperation and where price is secondary.

If your customer does not see value, and the differences between you and your competitors are clouded in his mind, your relationship is probably more like that of the vendor. We oftentimes think of the visual of a vending machine. If two vending machines were sitting side by side one selling Coke for $1.00 a can and the other for $1.50, who in their right mind would buy a can from the more expensive machine (unless you lived in Bel Air, then you'd buy the more expensive can and brag to all your friends)? If there are no perceived differences between products, we will always buy the lowest price option.

When a salesperson is treated as a vendor, he needs to look in the mirror and ask what he may be doing that contributes to this perception. For instance, if you are always leading with price, is it any wonder that price is the main focus? Or if you don't ask the right questions and tailor your solution to the customer's needs, do you really deserve to be treated as anything other than a vendor?

Putting Sales Methodology and the Sale Process into Practice

How do you elevate perception when more and more the customer wants to focus on price? This is where salesmanship comes into play, and this is where real salespeople (vs. order takers) earn their big commissions. Top performers recognize the importance of elevating customer perception in every interaction they have with a customer or prospect. Along with that, top performers qualify the opportunity to determine if this deal is something worth taking their time to try to elevate perception.

 TIP *We know there are some deals we should just walk away from. Top performers have the courage to do so.*

Let's look at some key areas that, if you focus on them, can elevate perception and ultimately help you close (or retain) more business.

Plan Like a General

General George Patton once said, "A good solution applied with vigor now is better than a perfect solution applied ten minutes later." A good solution, or a plan, is critical when determining battle strategies. The same can be said for selling. Top performers develop a plan for how they are going to hit their annual sales goal. They break that goal up into quarters and months.

They then look at the key activities that are going to drive this number and set activity-based goals for themselves. Success in sales is a mix of the right activity, the right number of opportunities to be working on, and the right close ratio. The trick is that the mix of these metrics is different for each of us.

Top performers know their metrics and adhere to them. High performers start with a territory plan, and they bucket opportunities A, B, and C. They then make sure they are applying the proper coverage strategy based on the quality of the opportunity. They then take their "A" accounts and develop a thorough account plan that points them to the key strategies they need to deploy. An account plan may contain multiple opportunities. Each of these opportunities has a plan for how they are going to win this business.

Overprepare for Each Customer Interaction

In sales, too many salespeople take the "gunslinger" mentality to meetings with customers and prospects. They think, "I've been selling for fifteen years; I pretty much already know what my customers need."

Consider a competitive selling situation. Vendor A shows up for an initial meeting and spends time asking the standard product-specific questions, which are right off of his company's standard needs analysis. Prior to Vendor B's meeting with the prospect, Vendor B researches the prospect thoroughly, uncovering interesting points pertaining to the prospect's business direction. Vendor B begins his meeting by demonstrating this understanding with some salient questions. If you were the customer, what would be your perception of Vendor A and Vendor B? Which company would you like to do business with?

 TIP *The best salespeople recognize the importance of preparation and make sure that their preparation includes researching what the customer's business is, what the customer's key business drivers look like, and the biggest challenges facing the customer's business.*

Be a Better Builder of Relationships

Have you ever won some business when you didn't have the best product or the best price? We hope the answer is yes. If you have been selling long enough, you have likely won a lot of business because you have built the best relationships. To the degree that you are able to build relationships with people who want you to win, you will be successful regardless of the sales methodology you use! This is such a critical point, and yet it amazes us that most salespeople do not spend time developing coaches or they under-utilize the coaches they already have.

Most of us would prefer to do it our way and not ask for help. You could write an entire book on how to cultivate coaching relationships. The value of the coach is critical especially in larger deals and longer, more complex sales cycles. Why? Think about all that a coach can do for you if you only asked. A coach can help you better understand the organizational structure of his company, who the key players are, and introduce you to other potential coaches. A coach can elevate you to higher levels of the organization by introducing you to key executives, provide you with competitive insight, preview your business presentations, and help with your overall account strategy. All you have to do is be willing to ask for help and listen! Be willing to let someone "coach" you. If you grasp this simple but powerful strategy, the probability of winning goes up immensely.

Make a Personal Impact

In this brief chapter, we have tried to focus on the selling skills and strategies that can really make a difference. Are you seeing a pattern here? Your level of preparation, your desire to want to focus on the customer's business, and your ability to build better relationships are just a few examples of the things you can do to elevate customer perception. Some of best strategies are the simplest:

- **Attire and appearance:** This is not to say that the best dressed is going to win. The more important question is: are you appropriately dressed? A dark suit with a starched white shirt may create the wrong perception in some situations. Do your homework and know how to dress to create the right impression.

- **Written communication:** It is true when they say the "devil is in the details." While a typo here or there can be forgiven, there are some customers who view poor grammar as a sign of a weak salesperson. Make sure all written communication is thoroughly proofed.

- **Integrity:** People don't buy from people they don't trust. Avoid making unrealistic statements about your product/service performance that you cannot substantiate. The customer will see right through this, and while he may not call you on it, the perception you have now created is indelible.

Conclusion

There was nothing earth shattering or revolutionary in the strategies we have discussed in this chapter, and that has really been our point throughout this discussion. There is no new battle strategy that is going to differentiate you from your competitors. It comes down to you and your ability to execute more effectively. You can use the same driver as pro golfer Rory McIlroy, but we guarantee you he knows how to execute his swing in such a way that he is going to put that ball eighty yards further down the fairway, and in the fairway, almost every time. Find an approach that includes the concepts discussed in these pages and learn to execute better than everyone else. How? Practice, repeatedly practicing over and over again.

Think back to when you were a kid in school. Whether you played sports or were in the band or in theater productions, what percent of your time did you spend practicing versus performing? We are guessing it was a mix of about 95 percent practice to 5 percent performance. What happens the minute you get out of school and into the business world? Unfortunately, for too many, the practice time goes away and they spend all their time performing or more likely "winging it." As we discussed in the motivation chapter, being really good at something comes at a price (e.g., practice time). The question to ask yourself is: are you willing to pay the price that it takes to get better?

CHAPTER 10

FINAL THOUGHTS ON TOP PERFORMANCE: ADVICE FOR SELLING SUCCESS

From Chip

Like many of us, my professional career has included both ups and downs. I have been recognized as a top performer at many stages of my career. I have also underperformed and been worried about losing my job. In sales, we ride a roller coaster of awards and recognition, and failure and consequences. I find that those who succeed in this profession develop the ability to compartmentalize failure. Many great closers in major league baseball will tell you the most important attribute of a successful closer is a short memory. In other words, they are able to give up the game-winning hit in the ninth inning one day, and then step on the mound the next day and have the confidence to throw another pitch. Remember that, if you are not failing, you are probably not stepping outside of your comfort zone and growing as a person.

One attribute that has seemed to be a constant for me in the highs and lows of my career is my self-awareness. Fortunately, when I have been underperforming, no one has needed to light a fire under me to work harder. When I am not performing, I feel terrible and believe I am usually harder on myself than anyone else could be. This self-awareness has served me well as I have been able to understand my key areas of development and continue to work to improve on them.

I have also benefited greatly from feedback from colleagues, bosses, mentors, and clients. The old saying that "feedback is a gift" is tested when you hear things that you don't want to hear about yourself. I will always remember a time in my career when I was struggling and I decided to ask a few colleagues I admired for feedback on my skills as a presenter/trainer. What I received back was very thorough and very critical. My first reaction was disappointment. I was disappointed that they felt this way about my skill set. My second reaction was anger. I became angry with myself for having to wait for this feedback before acting. I used this anger to motivate myself to improve. I embraced their feedback, built a plan for my improvement, and stuck to that plan until I achieved my desired state. Remember that seeking out feedback can be one of the most valuable (and courageous) things you do. Those who provide that feedback will admire you for putting it into action.

Like many of the people we have depicted in this book, I never set out for a career in sales. I fell into my career, and it wasn't until I was years into my career that my career got into me. Now I am obsessed with it. I can't get enough of it. I share this with you to offer further hope that it is never too late to embrace your career and develop that sense of purpose. I find that too many of today's sales professionals, while competent, are just going through the motions, lacking purpose and passion behind what they are doing. There are great strategies in this book that can help you reignite that passion; I hope you give them a try.

Finally, while we have written this book for sales and account management professionals, I believe that most of the concepts discussed in this book apply to all professions. Being married to someone whom I consider to be a top-performing teacher, I see each day how her attitude and motivation toward her job and the kids she is teaching make a huge difference. There are top-performing airline pilots, engineers, dentists, waitresses, and, yes, locker room attendants. One of my objectives in writing this book is to show that we are able to go beyond sales professionals and demonstrate how the strategies discussed in this book are universal. With that in mind, if you see someone struggling in his or her profession, or in need of reigniting their career, lend that person your book, or better yet . . . buy a copy for your friend.

From Scott

I would like to offer my final thoughts utilizing two life experiences that reinforce two points: how critical the attribute of attitude is to success, both personally and professionally, and that no one is perfect.

"Fat, drunk, and stupid is no way to go through life, son."

DEAN VERNON WORMER TO FLOUNDER
IN THE MOVIE ANIMAL HOUSE

We were all in inspection mode. The colonel was one Marine away from me when he asked, "What is your third general order?"

"To walk my post in a military manner," the Marine began, but the words and his confidence faded quickly. The colonel turned away from him to stand directly in front of me.

"What is your third general order?"

I quickly followed suit and responded confidently, "To walk my post in a military manner keeping always on the alert and . . ." I couldn't remember the rest to save my life; my mind went blank.

The colonel was not happy as he moved on to the next individual in formation and asked him the same question.

This Marine stood straight and recited beautifully, "To walk my post in a military manner, keeping always on the alert and observing everything that takes place within sight or hearing."

The pleased inspecting officer then stepped in front of the next Marine in the formation and asked, "What is your second general order?"

The response was the same as the last one verbatim! The colonel was upset, to say the least. "I thought that was your third general order?"

The Marine didn't hesitate to answer. "No, sir, my third general order is to report all violations of orders I am instructed to enforce."

We were all wrong—even the colonel. Only one individual had the confidence, or the knowledge, to not follow the rest and to walk his own path.

Here is the point: As a Marine, the general orders were drilled into my memory bank. I should have known them, and I did know them. However, I didn't trust myself that I had the right answer. I wasn't confident so I followed someone blindly who didn't know. Too many times we do this in business—follow the wrong, least successful people! In selling, it is your job to know your products, how your company works, and how to move a customer through the buying process. If you don't know today, it is your responsibility to get that knowledge. More importantly, if you have prepared yourself to succeed and covered your bases, trust yourself to come up with the right answer or right strategy and follow it confidently.

Live as if You Are Going to Die

*"Remembering that I'll be dead soon is the most
important tool I've ever encountered to help
me make the big choices in life. Because almost
everything—all external expectations, all pride, all
fear of embarrassment or failure—these things just
fall away in the face of death, leaving only what is
truly important. Remembering that you are going
to die is the best way I know to avoid the trap of
thinking you have something to lose.
You are already naked. There is no reason
not to follow your heart."*

EXCERPT FROM STEVE JOBS'S FAMOUS JUNE 2005
COMMENCEMENT ADDRESS AT STANFORD UNIVERSITY

I do a lot of presentations. Some have been great and some not so good. Many years back when I was new to the training and consulting field, I was on a business trip to New York to meet with some senior leadership of a large financial institution, and I was pumped up. I knew this was a big opportunity and likely to make my entire year's financial objectives. I was not only prepared but anxious and maybe overly prepared.

After a restless night of sleep, I arrived at the prospect's office early, at 7:00 a.m. (I am obviously not a New Yorker). The meeting didn't start until 9:00 a.m. When I was ushered into the meeting room, the senior executive team was waiting, some sitting around the large mahogany conference table, others being conferenced in by phone. This was my big moment.

After setting up my presentation, I began, "Gentlemen, I am excited to share what I believe to be a great business fit between our companies." Unfortunately, that was the best part of the presentation because it all went downhill from there.

I was so bad that I actually had an out-of-body experience watching myself fail. I broke every rule, written or unwritten, about effective presentations. I turned my back on the audience and spoke to my PowerPoint presentation. I was educating them versus trying to persuade them. I was rigid, not authentic. My mind had an internal argument with itself saying essentially, "You are failing here!" If I could have stopped right there, packed my bags, and left in the middle of it, I would have. But, that's a little conspicuous. I finished and walked out of the room with my tail between my legs.

Obviously, I did not get the deal, but worse than that, for the next couple of months, I was paralyzed with fear about reliving that presentation. What if it happened again? What if I look like a clown again in my next presentation? What if the audience were larger and I was a keynote presenter at a national conference? I had had a bad experience that I could not shake from my memory, and it was impacting my confidence—and presenting is what I do for a living!

Prior to my next presentations, I leveraged both positive self-talk and positive imaging: seeing myself doing a great job. Everything worked until right up to my introduction, when fear would strike me like the plague.

I needed a strategy to deal with the residual effects of that New York presentation, or it would impact my life indefinitely.

Then it hit me.

Why worry? I could die tomorrow.

Not a new concept, not a fatalistic view of my world, but a revolutionary strategy for me to deal with that paralyzing fear.

"I could die tomorrow."

I repeated the phrase over and over to myself prior to making presentations. What a concept: This might be my last day on Earth! Suddenly, I was able to put a new spin, a fresh perspective, on life. Others were fighting the good fight. Others really could die from accidents and illness.

No matter how this presentation turned out, it wasn't going to kill me. This thought process allowed me to take significant risks such as telling a story or a joke that the audience might enjoy and value rather than staying on script when presenting. Would these people remember me or what I presented to them in a year or two? Probably not. So why worry over something that didn't matter in the grand scheme of things? They'd either accept my presentation or they wouldn't. And I'd go on with other things, spend time with my family, eat my next meal.

Key point: Enjoy life. Realize that bad life experiences typically do not kill you. Whether presenting in front of a group, selling to senior-level decision makers, or making cold calls, have a mantra that you can utilize to put you at ease and put everything into perspective, something that will have a positive impact on your optimism and confidence.

> *"Twenty years from now, you will be more disappointed by the things you didn't do than the one you did do. So throw off the bowline. Sail away from the safe harbor. Catch the trade winds in your sails. Explore. Dream. Discover."*
>
> MARK TWAIN

We all like our routine. We like maintaining our comfort levels and status quo. We do what's expected of us and nothing more. We follow the wide path to small rewards when we could have so much more.

The average life expectancy for males at the time of this writing is seventy-seven. This means I only have about twenty-eight good years left! We all know that as time continues, the speed at which it accelerates is mind-boggling.

Don't follow the path of least resistance and never challenge the status quo. Go against the grain of convention. Chances are you'll discover more confidence, more wonderment, more love, and definitely more experiences.

So live and experience life.

Take as many risks as you can.

Enjoy the moment.

RESOURCES

Garfield, Charles. *Peak Performance.* New York: Warner Books, 1985.

Goleman, Daniel. *Working with Emotional Intelligence.* New York: Bantam, 1998, 2000.

Peoples, David. *Presentations Plus: David Peoples' Proven Techniques.* New York: John Wiley & Sons, Inc., 1992.

Peoples, David. *Selling to the Top.* New York: John Wiley & Sons, Inc., 1993.

Schwartz, Tony, and Jim Loehr. *Power of Full Engagement.* New York: Free Press, 2003.

Seligman, Martin. *Learned Optimism.* New York: Knopf, 1991.

NOTES

Chapter 2

University of Minnesota study on presentation skills. From David Peoples, *Presentations Plus: David Peoples' Proven Techniques* (John Wiley & Sons, Inc., 1992).

Chapter 4

Martin Seligman's positive thinking study at Met Life. From Martin Seligman, *Learned Optimism* (Knopf, 1991).

Vince Lombardi on confidence, www.vincelombardi.com/number-one.html.

Impact of negativity. From Martin Seligman, *Learned Optimism* (Knopf, 1991).

David McClelland on self-esteem. From Daniel Goleman, *Working with Emotional Intelligence* (Bantam, 1998, 2000).

Coach Herb Brooks's "Miracle" speech. From the movie *Miracle on Ice,* www.imdb.com.

Minnesota Vikings great John Randle and Randall McDaniel. From "John Randle: From Nothing to Canton" by Mark Craig, *Minneapolis StarTribune*, August 5, 2010.

Jack LaLanne seventieth birthday story. Sourced from www.jacklalanne.com/jacks-adventures/feats-and-honors.php.

Chapter 5

Modern Survey's latest study of the US workforce confirms a shift in the drivers of engagement. From www.modernsurvey.com/register-spring-2012-nns.

Sixty percent of customers say no four times before saying yes; 92 percent of salespeople give up after the fourth no. From David Peoples, *Presentations Plus: David Peoples' Proven Techniques* (John Wiley & Sons, Inc., 1992).

Chapter 6

Are people born top performers? From Charles Garfield, *Peak Performance* (Warner Books, 1985).

Business studies have found that top performers only achieve 50 percent of their goals. From Daniel Goleman, *Working with Emotional Intelligence* (Bantam, 1998, 2000).

Chapter 7

Study by Achieve Global breaks down the factors most critical to customers. From research by Achieve Global as presented at the Strategic Account Managers Association, www.strategicaccounts.org.

Study by the Forum Corporation on reasons why customers leave. From research by Forum as presented at the Strategic Account Managers Association, www.strategicaccounts.org.

INDEX

drinking problem
  impact on attitude 56
drive 84, 87, 91
driving forces 93–98, 139
  strategies for strengthening
    97–98

effectiveness
  true cost of 14
effectiveness bubble 9–10
energy
  managing 53
Erkel, Bob 85–86
executive power nap 53, 55
exercise
  impact on attitude 54

fear of failure 80, 96
Ferris Bueller's Day Off 88
Forbes, B.C. 18
Fromm, Erich 34

Gandhi, Mahatma 44
Gardner, Chris 108
Garfield, Charles 103
goals
  activity vs. outcome 99
goal setting 80, 99–100, 137,
    140
  S.M.A.R.T. 112–113
  tips 99
Goleman, Daniel 34
gratitude
  and motivation 98
Gray, Albert 77
Green, Dennis 60

Hubbard, Elbert 73

Insurance selling 86
integrity 14, 24, 25
  barriers to 122
  calendar 127
  corporate 122
  critical behaviors of 26
  damages to personal integrity
    123–126
  importance of 117–133,
    140–141
  personal 123, 141
  professional 123, 141
  sabotaging professional
    integrity 126–128, 151
  strategies for increasing
    130–131
investment
  in your sales career 84, 89

Jackson, Reggie 87
Jobs, Steve 160
Jordan, Michael 62, 64–65, 87
journaling 111, 115, 140

King Jr., Martin Luther 1

LaLanne, Jack 57
Learned Optimism 44, 46, 50
learning styles 65
Leno, Jay 129
Lincoln, Abraham 85
listening
  effective 128–129

ABOUT THE AUTHORS

SCOTT ANDERSON AND CHIP KUDRLE are managing partners of Diamond Performance Group. Scott and Chip have spent their entire careers—more than twenty-five years—selling, managing salespeople, and providing sales consulting, training, and coaching to some of the biggest and best sales organizations in the world. They have worked with leading organizations including 3M, IBM, Cargill, UnitedHealth Group, Carlson Companies, Andersen Windows, Wells Fargo, FIS, Microsoft, and Hewlett-Packard. They have authored numerous articles on sales effectiveness and are sought after speakers for both associations and national sales meetings. They both reside in the Twin Cities of Minneapolis/St. Paul.

Made in the USA
Charleston, SC
13 July 2013